The New York Times

READY, SET, SOLVE! CROSSWORDS
75 Puzzles to Test Your Speed and Challenge Your Mind

Edited by Will Shortz

ST. MARTIN'S GRIFFIN ⚏ NEW YORK

The New York Times

READY, SET, SOLVE! CROSSWORDS

My Time: _____ min

Beginner: 20 min   Intermediate: 12 min   Expert: 6 min

ACROSS

1 Part of a molecule
5 Supply-and-demand subj.
9 Pepsi and RC
14 Prom night transportation
15 Furry tunneler
16 Face-to-face exams
17 Alda of "What Women Want"
18 Othello's false friend
19 White-plumed wader
20 Profanity, e.g.
23 2007 film "___ and the Real Girl"
24 "Bonanza" star Greene
25 Sit behind bars
28 Memorial designer Maya ___
29 Cowboy boot attachment
32 Madonna title role
33 Flies off the handle
35 Mail carrier's beat: Abbr.
36 1995 Woody Allen comedy
39 Number before "ignition . . . liftoff!"
40 Bank robber's job
41 Dressed to the ___
42 Arctic floater
44 Suffix with meth-
45 "No Exit" playwright
46 Becomes frayed
48 Hand protector
49 Classic "Jeopardy!" category
54 Henhouse perch
55 Earthenware jar
56 College in New Rochelle, N.Y.
57 From days of yore

58 Bring up, as children
59 Be certain about
60 Saltine brand
61 Home of the invaders in Wells's "The War of the Worlds"
62 Snaky swimmers

DOWN

1 Self-pitying cry
2 Pinball foul
3 Sharif of "Doctor Zhivago"
4 Monument carved from a single stone
5 Settler from a foreign land
6 Snowman's eyes
7 Olympic gymnast Korbut
8 Nighttime advertising sign, maybe

9 ___ de Lion, epithet for Richard I
10 Church hymn accompaniers
11 Easily read type
12 Away from the wind
13 Lander at J.F.K., once
21 Football's Broadway Joe
22 Dead duck
25 Brit's service discharge
26 Sheeplike
27 Golfer named A.P. Male Athlete of the Year four times
28 Senior moment, e.g.
30 Pure-and-simple
31 Witherspoon of "Walk the Line"
33 Cloudburst

34 Beethoven specialty
37 Have a hankering
38 Off-road two-wheeler
43 Gird oneself
45 Indian instruments
47 Prudential rival
48 Grinding tooth
49 Extremity of the earth
50 "Not guilty," for one
51 Companionless
52 Hydroxyl-carbon compound
53 Toothed tools
54 Peri Gilpin's "Frasier" role

by Harvey Estes

My Time: _____ min

Beginner: 20 min   Intermediate: 12 min   Expert: 6 min

ACROSS

1 John ___, host of "America's Most Wanted"
6 "Jeopardy!" whiz Jennings
9 "Hey, you!"
13 ___ 2600 (classic video game console)
14 St. Louis landmark
15 Voice above a tenor
16 Appetizer with sweet and sour sauce
18 Gorilla watcher Fossey
19 Frightful female
20 Puccini heroine
21 Cheerful
22 Take turns
24 Dangler on a suitcase
26 Deadly long-tailed fish
28 Where you might get into hot water?
31 Schiaparelli of fashion
34 Cigarette substance
35 Interlocks
37 Bride's bounty
39 Meadow
41 Bird on birth announcement cards
42 Comes about
44 Wrigley's product
46 S. & L. conveniences
47 All U.S. senators until 1922
48 Monotonous voice
51 Birds flying in V's
53 Has confidence in
56 Beverly Sills and others
58 Young cod for dinner
60 F.D.R. job-creating measure: Abbr.
62 "Famous" cookie maker
63 Gangly guy
65 Fruit from a palm
66 "Don't hurt me!," e.g.
67 Straight up
68 Laid off, as workers
69 Wood in archery bows
70 Copenhageners, e.g.

DOWN

1 Do the laundry
2 Even, on the leaderboard
3 Slow, in symphonies
4 ___ Lanka
5 Merely suggest
6 Ray who created the McDonald's empire
7 Custardy dessert
8 Rink org.
9 City where Galileo taught
10 Goliath's undoing
11 Baseball's Musial
12 Broadway award
14 Weapons stash
17 "Oh, I see"
21 Eyelid nuisances
23 Romanov rulers
25 River blocker
27 One of the Allman Brothers
29 Straight-to-curly transformation, informally
30 Poses questions
31 Dutch city with a cheese market
32 Oral tradition
33 Make-or-break election bloc
36 Does' mates
38 Sí and oui
40 Home of the von Trapp family
43 Bro's sibling
45 Lamebrain
49 Get cozy
50 Prodded gently
52 Lessened, as pain
54 11- or 12-year-old
55 Rocket's realm
56 1920s art movement
57 Giant-screen theater
59 Backstage bunch
61 Tiny tunnelers
63 Mata Hari, for one
64 Top half of a bikini

by Lynn Lempel

My Time: _____ min

Beginner: 20 min   Intermediate: 12 min   Expert: 6 min

ACROSS
1. ___ mater
5. Letter-shaped structural piece
9. Lesser-played half of a 45
14. Elementary particle
15. Vex
16. Gucci alternative
17. Upstate New York city and spa
20. Remote areas
21. Imp
22. Head for
23. The boondocks
24. Honeymooners' destination
28. Alternative to .com or .edu
29. Fix, as brakes
30. Jacob's twin
34. Track events
36. Asian New Year
37. Leaves port
38. Bygone U.S. gas brand
39. Mother ___, 1979 Peace Nobelist
41. Napkin's place
42. Former president of Harvard
45. Kodak, Pentax and Nikon
48. The "L" in S. & L.
49. Is wild about
50. Mythical island that sank into the sea
54. Comic who played Robin Williams's son in "Mork & Mindy"
56. Auto route from Me. to Fla.
57. 1930s migrant
58. Smell ___ (be suspicious)
59. Groups of spies
60. Fails to keep pace
61. Without: Fr.

DOWN
1. "I ___ sorry!"
2. Hawaiian cookout
3. Homeowners' burdens
4. Like clocks with hands
5. Shipment to a steel mill
6. Home of the Cowboys, familiarly
7. "Sad to say . . ."
8. ___ judicata
9. Spread out ungracefully
10. Isle of Man's locale
11. Rumba or samba
12. Mystery writer's award
13. Swiss city on the Rhine, old-style
18. Dwellers along the Volga
19. Working stiff
23. French city where Jules Verne was born
24. Alaskan city where the Iditarod ends
25. Angers
26. Raises or lowers a hem, say
27. Passionate
31. Time before talkies
32. Banned orchard spray
33. Letter carriers' grp.
35. Broad-minded
37. Pago Pago resident
39. Garbage
40. Besmirches
43. Mountain ridges
44. Powerful rays
45. Louisianan of French descent
46. Get ___ of one's own medicine
47. Pre-stereo recordings
50. Paul who sang "Put Your Head on My Shoulder"
51. Tiny branch
52. Tehran's home
53. Concordes, briefly
55. "You've got mail" co.

by Richard Chisholm

My Time: _____ min

Beginner: 20 min   Intermediate: 12 min   Expert: 6 min

ACROSS

1 Doorframe parts
6 Chinese-born American architect
11 Be a pugilist
14 Bide one's time for
15 Manicurists' concerns
16 Electrical unit
17 One who's always up for a good time
19 Coastal inlet
20 Out of bed
21 ___ Aviv
22 In the near future
23 Prefix with -lithic
24 ___ of students
26 President before D.D.E.
27 Background check for a lender
32 Jay-Z and Timbaland
35 Atop, poetically
36 ___ Speedwagon
37 Horizontally
38 Musical transitions
40 "What was ___ do?"
41 Bulls, rams and bucks
43 Goes to
44 Long, long sentence
47 "I know what you're thinking" claim
48 Mississippi's Trent
49 BlackBerry, e.g., in brief
52 Unretrievable
54 Illustration, for short
55 Husband of Isis
58 April 15 org.
59 Light hauler
61 Sgt., e.g.
62 Didn't go out for dinner
63 Gift recipient
64 Floppy rabbit feature
65 Issues an advisory
66 Edgar Bergen's Mortimer ___

DOWN

1 Where the Pokémon craze originated
2 Cognizant (of)
3 Nintendo brother
4 Kibbles 'n ___
5 Eyelid woe
6 Holiday ___
7 Drink that often comes with an umbrella
8 Olive stuffing
9 Airline to Ben-Gurion
10 Nantucket, e.g.: Abbr.
11 Bruce Springsteen's first hit
12 Akron's home
13 Marvel mutant superhero
18 Big name in fairy tales
22 Egyptian viper
25 Actor Harris and others
26 Regarding this point
27 TV's "___ Sharkey"
28 Send again
29 Place that often has picnic tables
30 Hollow-stemmed plant
31 Flip
32 Fence part
33 Play's start
34 "Nutty" role for Jerry Lewis
39 ___ Xers
42 Worker with genes or film
43 Bit of land in a river
45 Superlative suffix
46 Brenda Lee's "___ Around the Christmas Tree"
49 Trim, as branches
50 Kitchen gizmo
51 Questioned
52 Word that can follow the starts of 17-, 27-, 44- and 59-Across
53 Killer whale
54 Sandwich bread
56 Norms: Abbr.
57 Fe, to chemists
59 Furry foot
60 Little ___ (tots)

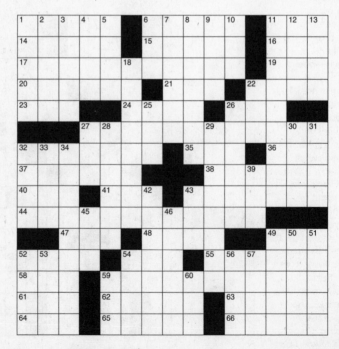

by Mark Sherwood

My Time: _____ min

Beginner: 20 min   Intermediate: 12 min   Expert: 6 min

ACROSS

1 Oodles
6 Wide as the ocean
10 Huffed and puffed
14 Seoul's land
15 Diva's song
16 Jacob's first wife
17 A magnet attracts it in a physics experiment
19 Between twice and never
20 Grand Coulee, e.g.
21 County seat NNW of Oklahoma City
22 Relieve
24 At a tilt
26 Praise
27 Tire filler
28 Divorces
32 Locale for a New York diva
35 What the number of birthday candles signifies
36 Olden times
37 Jinxes
38 Snooper's org.
39 Tomato-hitting-the-floor sound
40 Speed skater Heiden
41 Bamboozle
42 Sales pitches
43 Zilch
45 Carry the day
46 Crazy-sounding bird
47 Freighters' freights
51 One with a hook, line and sinker
54 Stuporous sleep
55 Doc's picture producer
56 Java neighbor
57 Star's marquee position
60 Genesis garden
61 Tall tale teller
62 Have a meal at home
63 Orange-flavored powdered drink
64 "Born Free" lioness
65 Medicinal amounts

DOWN

1 On the ___ (going to pot)
2 Deep pink
3 Enticing smell
4 TV room
5 Two-point plays in football
6 Legitimate
7 Parched
8 Envy or gluttony
9 Event before moving
10 Pre-transfusion procedure
11 Gave for a while
12 "To ___ his own"
13 Amusement park shout
18 Lifeless
23 "Yes, madame"
25 Some verbal abuse
26 Women's links org.
28 Paragon of virtue
29 One and only
30 ___ Mountains, Europe/Asia separator
31 Four-footed friends
32 Next
33 Medal winner for bravery
34 Escape route
38 Nickel or dime
39 Shot up, as inflation
41 Gleeful laugh
42 Hindu teacher
44 Misery
47 King ___ (dangerous snake)
48 Skips
49 Old TV comic Kovacs
50 Leo and Libra
51 Help illegally
52 Zilch
53 "Galveston" crooner Campbell
54 Inspectors of fin. books
58 "Black gold"
59 Neighbor of a Vietnamese

by Lynn Lempel

My Time: _____ min

Beginner: 20 min   Intermediate: 12 min   Expert: 6 min

ACROSS

1 Peeling knives
7 "See ya"
10 Katie Couric's network
13 Kansas city where Dwight Eisenhower grew up
15 Symbol of sturdiness
17 High hit behind the catcher, say
18 Do surgery (on)
19 End of a school Web address
20 Salves
22 "My life __ open book"
23 Ward off
26 Safety item for a tightrope walker
27 Pep rally shout
28 Refused
30 Tallied up
33 Neurologist or orthopedist
36 Graceful swimmer
38 Nuptial agreement
39 Spotty
41 Tidy savings
43 Miss. neighbor
44 __ of Man
46 Paths from here to there
47 Stretchy fabric
49 Self-assurance
51 Family
52 Vegetable that rolls
53 Looks to be
57 Treble's counterpart
59 Thorny parts of roses
61 III + IV
62 Miss terribly

64 Theory of the universe, or a hint to the starts of 17-Across and 7-, 10-, 35- and 40-Down
67 Scene at a natural history museum
68 Observed secretly
69 Summer hrs. in D.C.
70 One doing leg. work
71 Derisive looks

DOWN

1 Post or Trib
2 Residence
3 Shred
4 Aide to Santa
5 Old auto inits.
6 Rebuff
7 Prosperous place
8 Kennel cries

9 __ out (barely make)
10 Extreme effort at weight loss
11 Alpha, __, gamma . . .
12 Glimpsed
14 Twisty-horned antelope
16 Musical chord
21 Eye part
24 "Cómo __ usted?"
25 Vientiane native
27 Abductors' demands
29 Eye part
31 Periphery
32 Lady and the Tramp, e.g.
33 Start a card game
34 Air France destination
35 Skilled marksman

37 Aviation-related prefix
40 Baloney
42 Inside of a paper towel roll
45 Sporting sword
48 One heeding the alarm clock
50 Symbols of meekness
54 Dodge
55 Petty
56 + and −
57 Ordered
58 Carbolic __
59 A few
60 Nurses a drink
63 Lead-in to fetched or sighted
65 Card game with knocking
66 Spelling competition

by Lynn Lempel

My Time: _____ min

Beginner: 20 min   Intermediate: 12 min   Expert: 6 min

ACROSS

1 Bay State sch.
6 Juicy fruits
11 Target of many a boxing blow
14 Sophomore's grade
15 Old Testament prophet
16 "It's no ___!"
17 Good sign on a highway
19 Reverse of NNW
20 Dollar or Budget competitor
21 Like the season before Easter
23 Floated gently in the air
26 7 on a grandfather clock
28 Prefix with potent
29 Use a rasp on
30 Comment on, as in a margin
32 Expected
33 Org. for the humane treatment of pets
35 Bobby of the N.H.L.
36 Alcoholics Anonymous has 12 of them
39 Once around a track
40 Catnip and fennel
43 Safe box opener
44 White ___ (termites)
46 Cousin of a Keogh, briefly
47 Arizona's Petrified Forest dates from this period
50 Optimistic
53 Sups
54 "___ luck?"
55 Heavy hammer
56 Bear witness
58 Consequently
59 Fr. holy woman
60 Good sign on a candy box
66 Dark time, in poetry
67 Vice President Burr
68 Weights abroad, informally
69 Scores in the end zone, for short
70 Velocity
71 Appears

DOWN

1 Western tribe
2 "___ in Black," Will Smith film
3 &
4 Layers
5 Acted rudely while in a line, maybe
6 Academics' degrees
7 High's opposite
8 Grp. that entertains the troops
9 Magician in Arthurian legend
10 Hot Japanese drink
11 Good sign on a car trunk
12 Concurrence
13 Ineffectual one, slangily
18 Helpers
22 ___ Dame
23 Bankrolls
24 Be next to
25 Good sign on a lawn
26 Good sign at a motel
27 Not well-put
31 "That feels gooood!"
34 "Above the fruited ___"
37 Kind of porridge
38 The "S" in CBS: Abbr.
41 Boast
42 Fill the stomach of
45 Dish often served with 10-Down
47 Group of cups and saucers
48 Squealed (on)
49 Despotic ruler
51 Sets (down)
52 Nickname for Elizabeth
57 Places to be pampered
58 Manage, as a bar
61 Anger
62 Actress Caldwell
63 ___ de France
64 Suffix with official
65 Twisty curve

by Robert Dillman

My Time: _____ min

Beginner: 20 min   Intermediate: 12 min   Expert: 6 min

ACROSS

1 Money hoarder
6 Frosts, as a cake
10 Notre ___
14 Houston ballplayer
15 Former ruler of Iran
16 Fusses
17 Poker player's dream
19 Revivalists
20 Suspicious
21 Gown fabric
22 Faucet
26 Soup ingredient
28 K.F.C. founder, with "the"
30 King Kong, e.g.
31 Foray
32 Delete from a disk
35 Nutritional abbr.
38 Out of sorts feeling (and a hint to the starts of 17-, 26-, 49- and 59-Across)
42 Prof.'s degree
43 Opening bets
44 Coffee holders
45 Long-distance inits.
46 Run
49 Parachutist
54 Egg dish
55 With nothing added
56 Ping or zing
58 Swedish diva Jenny
59 Makeup applicator
64 "Puppy Love" singer Paul
65 Ye ___ Curiosity Shoppe
66 Magical wish granter
67 Trueheart of the comics
68 Paths
69 Glue

DOWN

1 Spoil
2 Prefix with -metric
3 Sow's pen
4 Pitcher's stat.
5 Deodorant type
6 ___ of Capri
7 Butter maker
8 Snap course
9 "Quiet!"
10 River in a Strauss waltz
11 Fred's dancing sister
12 Money, in slang
13 German industrial city
18 Celebration
21 Laid-back sort
22 Toss out
23 Simmer, as eggs
24 Trojan War epic
25 Mount Olympus dwellers
27 Flower holder
29 Took off
33 Rd. or hwy.
34 "I get it," humorously
35 The "R" of R.F.D.
36 Al ___ (not too soft)
37 Strong point
39 Have dinner at home
40 "As advertised ___!"
41 Tackle box item
45 Nike rival
47 Sit for a photo
48 Come into view
49 Water balloon sound
50 "A Fish Called Wanda" Oscar winner
51 Americans, to Brits
52 ___ Gay (W.W. II plane)
53 Rambunctious
57 Middle of March
59 Comic book punch sound
60 Get-up-and-go
61 Numero ___
62 Repair
63 Hardly macho

by Marjorie Berg

My Time: _____ min

Beginner: 20 min   Intermediate: 12 min   Expert: 6 min

ACROSS
1 Baby's first word, in Italy
6 Commercials
9 Touches
14 Skip ___ (lose tempo)
15 Tennis do-over
16 Katmandu's land
17 ___ firma
18 Mai ___ (tropical drink)
19 "Yum!"
20 "Future Shock" author
23 Prefix with -lithic
24 Wetland
25 Antique restorer's efforts, for short
28 Late hunter of Nazi war criminals
34 Comedian Philips
35 Aria singer
36 Brewing coffee produces one
37 Designer Christian
39 Semesters
42 Muslim holy man
43 Shake hands (on)
45 Former senator Trent
47 ___ dye (chemical coloring)
48 "Sister Carrie" author
52 Airport schedule abbr.
53 The 1919 Treaty of Versailles concluded it: Abbr.
54 Directional suffix
55 Singing group suggested by the starts of 20-, 28- and 48-Across
61 Dragon Ball Z game company
64 ___ Solo of "Star Wars"

65 Actress Papas or Ryan
66 Thesaurus author
67 Superlative suffix
68 Girlish laugh
69 Bullwinkle, for one
70 Letter between pi and sigma
71 Actress Falco and namesakes

DOWN
1 ___ Hari
2 Brother of Cain and Seth
3 "___ Griffin's Crosswords"
4 Dolphins QB Dan
5 Finished
6 Choir voice
7 Like most users of sign language
8 Cadavers, slangily

9 Insect or radio part
10 Yogi, for one
11 FedEx competitor
12 Tit for ___
13 Crafty
21 Namely
22 Former auto executive Iacocca
25 Clarence of the Supreme Court
26 Kind of class for expectant mothers
27 Noisy shouting
28 Anesthetize, say
29 "Put me down as a maybe"
30 Tied down, as a boat
31 "___ changed my mind"
32 Country rocker Steve

33 Prefix with lateral
38 Old Olds car
40 "The ___ Squad" of '60s–'70s TV
41 Throat problem
44 First American to walk in space
46 Orkin target
49 Be in the red
50 Wealthier
51 Accustomed
55 ___ chic
56 Corned beef concoction
57 Absorbed by
58 Soda pop brand
59 Thigh/shin connector
60 Understands
61 Slot machine part
62 Excessively
63 In the past

by Michael Blake

My Time: _____ min

Beginner: 20 min   Intermediate: 12 min   Expert: 6 min

ACROSS

1 "___ upon a time . . ."
5 Like a score of 10 out of 10
10 Speedy
14 "Star Wars" princess
15 Dated yet trendy
16 Knowing of
17 "See you again!"
20 Longtime CBS and NBC newsman Roger
21 Touchdown destination
22 Blacktops
25 Tricky curves
27 Bud's partner in comedy
28 Had dinner
29 ___ B'rith
30 Coarse file
31 "Veni, vidi, vici" speaker
34 The "R" of NPR
37 "See you again!"
41 Henry Blake's rank on "M*A*S*H": Abbr.
42 Many IM recipients
44 Letterhead design
47 "___ Green" (Kermit the Frog song)
49 Snooze
50 In the style of
51 Mah-jongg pieces
53 Domineering
55 The dole
57 Chief Norse deity
59 "See you again!"
64 Suffix with sock
65 Ship-related
66 Lawman Wyatt
67 Former Cub ___ Sandberg
68 Entrap
69 Where "you can do whatever you feel," in a hit 1978 song

DOWN

1 Outdated
2 Recent: Prefix
3 The Reds, on scoreboards
4 Words on a Wonderland cake
5 Steamed
6 Muffle, as a sound
7 U.F.O. fliers
8 Kind of well
9 Michaels of "Saturday Night Live"
10 "Happy Days" cool cat, with "the"
11 Country north of Namibia
12 Dictation takers
13 Shredded
18 Greyhound vehicle
19 TV spots
22 Grp. funding 19-Down in campaigns
23 Just slightly
24 Swerve
26 "Nobody doesn't like" her, in a slogan
29 ___-a-brac
30 Stir up
32 Lindbergh's classic flight, e.g.
33 Fitting
35 Actress Cannon
36 "How was ___ know?"
38 Duke or earl
39 Restroom door word
40 Chapters in history
43 Austin Powers, e.g.
44 Perry Mason, e.g.
45 Clinton cabinet member Hazel
46 Gasoline unit
48 Weather map line
51 Tic-___-toe
52 Cattle branding tools
53 Lighter and pen maker
54 Perfectly pitched
56 A polar bear might be found on one
58 Valley
60 Actress Mendes
61 '60s conflict site
62 Tolkien creature
63 F.D.R. initiative

by Dave and Tracy Mackey

My Time: _____ min

Beginner: 20 min   Intermediate: 12 min   Expert: 6 min

ACROSS

1 Black-bordered news item
5 Anne of "Wag the Dog"
10 Dull-colored
14 Internet connection at a restaurant or airport
15 Fanfare
16 Seized vehicle
17 Snoop
19 Height: Prefix
20 Steak that a dog might end up with
21 "Huckleberry Finn" author
22 Wet mascara worry
25 Felix and Oscar, with "the"
28 Bathroom powder
30 Wyatt of the Wild West
31 Magazine V.I.P.'s
32 1980s video game with a maze
35 Down, usually, on a light switch
38 Carouse
42 Golf peg
43 Boxed stringed instrument
44 "___ solemnly swear . . ."
45 Ax or awl
47 Judicial assertion
49 Symbol of purity
54 Figure of speech
55 Wall art
56 Mutual of ___
58 "Gotcha," to a beatnik
59 Want ad heading . . . or a hint to the starts of 17-, 25-, 38- and 49-Across
64 Queue
65 More than steamed
66 March Madness org.
67 Brain readings, for short
68 Parceled (out)
69 Safecracker

DOWN

1 To have and to hold
2 Life story, for short
3 Conditions
4 Men's fashion accessory
5 Submarine sandwich
6 Commercial prefix with Lodge
7 Informed, with "in"
8 ___ Solo of "Star Wars"
9 Flight board info: Abbr.
10 Use, as past experience
11 CliffsNotes version
12 "___ Love," 1957 #1 hit by 13-Down
13 Singer Pat
18 Brusque
21 The Blue Jays, on a scoreboard
22 Rung
23 Furious with
24 Pitcher of milk?
26 John Donne's "___ Be Not Proud"
27 Went by dugout
29 Passover bread
33 Spicy dish that may have a fire-alarm rating
34 Encountered
36 ___-Lay (snack company)
37 At the end of one's patience
39 Take-home pay
40 Squirm
41 Capitol's top
46 Bird that hoots
48 Crevice
49 Photographer's request
50 Peep show flick
51 Circular gasket
52 Go ___ for (support in time of need)
53 Overact
57 Copied
59 Huck's raftmate
60 Metal from a mine
61 Sno-cone filler
62 Re-re-re-remind
63 Respond to a really bad joke, maybe

by Ken Bessette

My Time: _____ min

Beginner: 20 min   Intermediate: 12 min   Expert: 6 min

ACROSS

1 Bounce to the surface
6 Botch
10 Sports equipment
14 Belittle
15 Least bit
16 Present opener?
17 Free health and dental care, and then some
20 List of test answers
21 Aviates
22 Limerick or sonnet
23 Luke's twin sister in "Star Wars"
24 Price ___ pound
25 Math symbol for extraction of a root
30 Pilot's stat.
33 Warnings
34 Entree in a bowl with beef or lamb, say
36 Pelvic bones
37 Boat propeller
38 Clark's crush on "Smallville"
39 "Hey, come back a bit"
42 Enter en masse
44 Where pigs wallow
45 In limbo
47 Wood-shaping tool
48 Nays' opposites
49 Flair
52 Peppermint ___ of "Peanuts"
54 Sombrero, e.g.
57 Eyeglass option for different distances
60 Early state in the presidential campaign
61 Reclined
62 Major artery
63 The Big Board: Abbr.
64 Doe's mate
65 Winona of "Girl, Interrupted"

DOWN

1 Pitcher's faux pitch
2 New York theater award
3 One often needing a change
4 Take advantage of
5 "Couldn't be better!"
6 Pertaining to a son or daughter
7 Ear or leaf part
8 Four Corners-area Indians
9 Prohibition
10 Errand runner
11 Dubai dignitary
12 Six-legged scurriers
13 Move skyward
18 Fake identity
19 Occurrence
23 Bygone Italian coins
24 Tour grp.?
25 Monsoon occurrences
26 Apportion
27 God or goddess
28 Brainy
29 Suffix with bombard
30 Trailblazing video game maker
31 His tomb is in Red Square
32 Banjo sound
35 Hits hard
37 Lummox
40 Like 16 vis-à-vis 15, agewise
41 Turk's topper
42 Home viewing for a price
43 Subscription period, often
46 Loathing
47 Aquatic plant life
49 Pirouette
50 "Iliad" setting
51 Cries after being burned
52 H.S. junior's exam
53 Where most of Russia is
54 Group of buffalo
55 Prefix with chamber
56 Ruler before 31-Down
58 Ernie of the 24-Down
59 Silver screen star Myrna

by Lynn Lempel

My Time: _____ min

Beginner: 30 min   Intermediate: 15 min   Expert: 8 min

The answers at 17- and 51-Across and 11- and 24-Down can all be defined by the same missing three-letter word. What is it?

ACROSS

1 Keen-edged
6 Gave in
11 ___-a-cake
14 Chomping at the bit
15 Last Olds made
16 Corrida cheer
17 See blurb
19 Cooking spray brand
20 "When hell freezes over"
21 Grouch
23 Not exactly insightful
26 Gung-ho sort
27 Minty drinks
28 Greg's sitcom mate
30 Oklahoma Indians
31 Some earrings
32 Slugger's stat
35 Hershey confection
36 Pasta is loaded with them
37 Skier's transport
38 "I do"
39 Four-page sheet
40 An ex of the Donald
41 Martini garnishes
43 Shiny fabric
44 Regal fur
46 Brilliantly colored parrots
47 Actress Gaynor
48 Scarlett of Tara
50 "Evil Woman" band, for short
51 See blurb
57 Cornhusker State: Abbr.
58 Special talent
59 Fashionably old-fashioned
60 Batiking need
61 Doughboys
62 Thoroughly enjoy

DOWN

1 Trice, informally
2 "2001" computer
3 In the past
4 Counterpart of bus.
5 Engagement contracts, briefly
6 Cut up
7 "I cannot tell ___"
8 Zig or zag
9 Directional suffix
10 For whom Sandy Koufax pitched
11 See blurb
12 Texas shrine
13 Tantalize
18 Come clean, with "up"
22 Smash into
23 Belly button type
24 See blurb
25 Summer shirts
26 Nukes
27 Facetious
28 Day of "Pillow Talk"
29 Boxcar rider
31 In the pink
33 Farm bundles
34 Neighbor of Turkey
36 Place to moor
37 "Later"
39 Like a picky eater
40 Like much of Poe's work
42 Designer Claiborne
43 ___ Lee cakes
44 Make corrections to
45 Life of ___ (ease)
46 Some big trucks
48 Mideast sultanate
49 Bumpkin
52 ___ lark
53 Arthur of "The Golden Girls"
54 Hall-of-Famer Mel
55 Play about Capote
56 Toy with a string

by Alison Donald

My Time: _____ min

Beginner: 30 min   Intermediate: 15 min   Expert: 8 min

ACROSS

1 Like some petticoats
5 Own up (to)
10 Bank with significant deposits?
14 Award for "Hot L Baltimore"
15 Harness parts
16 Writer ___ Stanley Gardner
17 Teen's response to a parent's "No"
20 Somme summer
21 Greek war god
22 Novelist Joyce Carol ___
23 Blacken
24 Pumpkin pie ingredient
26 Outdated
29 Musical Count
30 "Encore!"
31 Forest in "As You Like It"
32 By way of
35 Teen's response to a parent's "No"
39 & 40 Change of government
41 1973 #1 hit "___ an American Band"
42 Basketball position
43 Gushed
45 Subject to legal damages
47 Like badly worn tires
48 Peter of "Casablanca"
49 "Howdy!"
50 Batman and Robin, e.g.
53 Teen's response to a parent's "No"
57 Window section
58 Power problem
59 Mideast V.I.P.
60 Narrow cut
61 Wheels for big wheels
62 Folk singer Seeger

DOWN

1 Ear or leaf feature
2 Be next to
3 Mention, as in a court opinion
4 To date
5 Couples' destination?
6 Prevent through intimidation
7 Pageant title
8 Country lodge
9 General on a Chinese menu
10 Malign
11 Steaming
12 Movie-set light
13 Plural suffix with auction or musket
18 "Aren't you the comedian?!"
19 Lugging
23 "Moonstruck" actress
24 Point from which there's nowhere to go but up
25 Depletes, with "up"
26 Meteor shooting across the sky, maybe
27 Aphrodite's domain
28 Sketched
29 Kennel club listing
31 Tennis great Agassi
32 Panorama
33 Memo phrase
34 Like some cheeses
36 "Absolutely!"
37 ___ surgeon
38 Had to hand it to?
42 January birthstone
43 What the teen wishes the parent would do instead
44 Land office map
45 Hometown-related
46 Tehran resident
47 "Ex-x-xactly!"
48 Kissers
49 Havoc
50 "It's your ___"
51 Military group
52 Nasty sort
54 Hi-speed connection
55 Non's opposite
56 With it, once

by Gail Grabowski

My Time: _____ min

Beginner: 30 min   Intermediate: 15 min   Expert: 8 min

ACROSS

1 Comment not to be taken seriously
5 ___ Marley's ghost in "A Christmas Carol"
10 Con game
14 Unwanted spots
15 Band together
16 Poi source
17 Response to a knock
19 29,035 ft., for Mt. Everest
20 Have a bawl
21 Designer label letters
22 Heap kudos on
24 "For instance . . ."
25 Empathize with
26 The important thing
31 A Chaplin
32 Sluggers' stats
33 Lhasa ___ (Tibetan dogs)
38 Doctor's query
41 Scattered about
42 Entre ___
43 Metropolitan ___
44 "Never!"
47 Some apartments
51 Uno + due
52 Apartment window sign
53 Kudrow of "Friends"
55 Mediterranean fruit
58 Both: Prefix
59 Discounter's pitch
62 Computer with an iSight camera
63 Have an ___ mystery
64 Plow pullers
65 Unit of force
66 Teammate of Snider and Hodges
67 Classic computer game set on a seemingly deserted island

DOWN

1 1975 Spielberg thriller
2 Eerie cave effect
3 One not associating with the likes of you?
4 Private eye, for short
5 Place to find auto parts
6 Have ___ with
7 Half of an E.P.A. mileage rating
8 Pony players' locale, in brief
9 Paging device
10 Incredible bargain
11 Where the San Andreas Fault is: Abbr.
12 "Ain't!" retort
13 Shaker's partner
18 Genesis patriarch
23 Convened again
24 "Can you believe this?" look
25 Come clean
26 Knocks the socks off
27 Alternative to a Twinkie
28 From the top
29 Steakhouse selections
30 Attach, in a way
34 Terrible twos, e.g.
35 Browse, as the Web
36 Sportscaster Hershiser
37 Hang around
39 Dickens's Drood
40 "Can I come out now?"
45 Armed conflict
46 Battleship shade
47 Sober
48 Rock opera with the song "Pinball Wizard"
49 Densely packed, in a way
50 Pour salt on, perhaps
53 Apollo's instrument
54 N.Y.S.E. debuts
55 Full of guile
56 Tees off
57 Fellow
60 Step on it
61 Soccer ___

by Alan Arbesfeld

My Time: _____ min

Beginner: 30 min   Intermediate: 15 min   Expert: 8 min

ACROSS

1 Sword handles
6 Worker's due
10 Wood-shaping tool
14 "One for My Baby" composer Harold
15 Horse course
16 One of nine in golf
17 "Merry Christmas" to the French
19 Antique autos
20 Tipple
21 Winter melon
23 "Atlas Shrugged" author Rand
24 Shooters' grp.
26 Genie holders
29 "Merry Christmas" to Danes
33 Spar verbally
36 "I can only __ much"
37 Sch. named for a televangelist
38 Life stories on film
40 Leak fixer
43 Toss in
44 Not e'en once
46 Inspiring sisters
47 "Merry Christmas" to Spaniards
51 "Lemon Tree" singer Lopez
52 Third after delta
53 "Pow!"
56 Federer and Nadal
59 Collected
62 Hgt.
64 "Merry Christmas" to Italians
66 Two capsules, perhaps
67 Terrier sounds
68 Animated ogre
69 Cold war superpower
70 Sectional, e.g.
71 Makeup maker Lauder

DOWN

1 Muslim pilgrim
2 Kitchen drawer?
3 Visit from the Blue Angels, maybe
4 Readying for a drive
5 Cold-shoulder
6 Hit the jackpot
7 Guacamole ingredient
8 Greek earth goddess
9 Architects' annexes
10 Car safety device
11 Prized positions
12 Menagerie
13 U.S.N.A. grad
18 TV's Warrior Princess
22 Thrilla in Manila boxer
25 It had a notable part in Exodus
27 Blender setting
28 Pronounces poorly
30 Waikiki welcome
31 Lively wit
32 Chat room chuckle
33 Sailor's behind
34 Bill tack-on
35 Piety
39 It has headquarters at N.Y.C.'s Time Warner Center
41 Thurman of "Dangerous Liaisons"
42 Spa treatments
45 Make balanced
48 "The nerve!"
49 Benzoyl peroxide target
50 "Rats!"
54 Split up
55 Knock-down-drag-out
57 Corp. recruits, often
58 Continental currency
60 Move gently
61 Apollo astronaut Slayton
62 Campus e-mail suffix
63 Acapulco article
65 Supersecretive intelligence org.

by Nancy Salomon

My Time: _____ min

Beginner: 30 min   Intermediate: 15 min   Expert: 8 min

ACROSS

1 "Mamma Mia" group
5 Play chauffeur
10 Money to help one through a tight spot
14 Either of two directing brothers
15 All gone, as dinner
16 Mayberry boy
17 Daydreamer's state
20 Directional suffix
21 A choir may stand on it
22 Good thing
23 Sailor, colloquially
24 Digit in binary code
25 Joseph Conrad novella
34 Edward who wrote the play "The Goat, or Who Is Sylvia"
35 Pastor's flock
36 Rebellious Turner
37 Vintage autos
38 Kind of club that's a hint to this puzzle's theme
39 Prefix with lock or knock
40 ___-cone
41 Colonial settlement
42 Bobby Orr, notably
43 Vocational school instruction
46 Superannuated
47 Ring outcome, briefly
48 ___ pants (multipocketed wear)
51 Room plus, in a hotel
54 "Don't ___"
57 Common employment benefit
60 Cleveland's lake
61 Enlarge a house
62 Men-only
63 "The World of Suzie ___"
64 Sierra ___, Africa
65 Certain vanity plate for husband-and-wife cars

DOWN

1 Suffer from a charley horse
2 Transvaal trekker
3 Vanilla ___
4 "What else?"
5 "Meet the Fockers" co-star, 2004
6 Hamelin's problem
7 "___ Jury" (Spillane novel)
8 Zig or zag
9 S.A.S.E., e.g.
10 Relax, as rules
11 Berkeley Breathed comic strip
12 Lieutenant
13 Fit snugly
18 Really hot under the collar
19 Like Lincoln, in physique
23 Uno + dos
24 Straight: Prefix
25 Hard on the ears
26 "Maria ___" (Dorsey tune)
27 ___ to mankind
28 Taken wing
29 Intimidate
30 Station with a show
31 The blahs
32 Participated temporarily, as with a band
33 Police con
38 Victuals
39 Florence's river
41 Letter-shaped opening for a bolt
42 Harley rider
44 Links bend
45 Bring into harmony
48 Stick of gum, e.g.
49 Prefix with -postale
50 Common Seattle forecast
51 Slaw or fries, e.g.
52 Reverse, on a PC
53 "The shoe ___ the other foot"
54 A couple of chips, maybe
55 Injury reminder
56 Purchases for a shindig
58 ___ 9000, sci-fi computer
59 Bit of air pollution

by Adam G. Perl

My Time: _____ min

Beginner: 30 min   Intermediate: 15 min   Expert: 8 min

ACROSS

1 Desktop folder, e.g.
5 John Candy's old comedy show
9 William of ___, known for his "razor"
14 Bay of Pigs locale
15 Rock's Mötley ___
16 He didn't give a damn
17 Fedora feature
18 Boot from office
19 Angora and merino
20 What you really saw?
23 Sonora snack
24 Pass by
28 What you really saw?
32 First secretary of homeland security
33 ___ Lingus
34 Quito's land: Abbr.
35 Co. that owns Parlophone records
36 Z's
40 Tolkien humanoid
41 Many want-ad offerings: Abbr.
43 Play for a sap
44 "I ___ amused!"
46 What you really saw?
50 "Super!"
51 N.R.A. part: Abbr.
52 What you thought you saw
58 Tiny hairs
61 "Scarface" star, 1932
62 Economy-___
63 Don't exist
64 Sidewalk stand drinks
65 Raison d'___

66 Sheriff's symbol
67 Abominable Snowman
68 Circus barker

DOWN

1 Minuteman, e.g.: Abbr.
2 Make perfect again
3 End piece?
4 "Hello" sticker
5 Burn with an iron
6 Defoe castaway
7 Keister
8 Challenge to Congress
9 Big Brother's creator
10 Bach work
11 Corp. V.I.P.
12 Turner Field locale: Abbr.
13 See 25-Down
21 Hall's singing partner
22 Pooped
25 With 13-Down, Pa. range
26 Grow sick of
27 Make into law
28 Part of a nun's habit
29 Blue-pencil wielder
30 Judge of sex and violence in films
31 Swarm member
32 Flinch, say
37 Peeved and showing it
38 Grp. helping those on shore leave
39 ___ hole in (corrodes)

42 Web recreation
45 Grade lowerers
47 Get wider
48 Refrigerator adornment
49 St. Francis's home
53 "If ___ be so bold . . ."
54 Pantyhose shade
55 Summon to court
56 Poet Pound
57 Fiddler's tune
58 It may have a medallion
59 Roth ___
60 Had charge of

by Malia Jackson and Noah Snyder

My Time: _____ min

Beginner: 30 min   Intermediate: 15 min   Expert: 8 min

ACROSS

1 Some charity fundraisers
6 Outspoken
11 Org. with a code
14 Singer Davis with the 1998 hit "32 Flavors"
15 Airplane seat choice
16 Old ___, London theater
17 Joie de vivre
19 Lab eggs
20 Accomplish
21 Star-related
23 Prank player
26 "South Park" kid
27 Preceder of Bell or shell
31 Speed-happy driver
33 Book in which the first Passover occurred
35 Castle protector
36 Middle-earth meanie
39 Teacher's charge
40 Paris's ___ Invalides
41 Colder and windier
43 "___ a Tramp" ("Lady and the Tramp" tune)
44 Singer Pinza
46 Popular setting for a wedding
47 Fantastically wonderful
50 Snare
51 Daughter of Czar Nicholas I or II
53 Arctic bird
55 Newswoman Katie
57 Diner sign filler
62 ___-la-la
63 Speaking manner
66 Go wrong
67 Proficient
68 O.K.
69 Newsman Koppel
70 Fix, as laces
71 This puzzle's theme

DOWN

1 ___ Strip (much-fought-over area)
2 British P.M. ___ Douglas-Home
3 Whip
4 Prefix with matter
5 Like wearing a seat belt, e.g.
6 Lombardy province or its capital
7 De-squeak
8 CBS forensic drama
9 "Our Gang" kid
10 Famous Virginia family
11 Lofty place for an academic
12 Pepsi vis-à-vis Coke
13 Symbol of justice
18 Racetracks
22 Bout decision
24 Didn't stay on
25 Kerfuffles
27 Part of M.I.T.: Abbr.
28 Highway toll unit
29 Its academy is in New London, Conn.
30 Some E.R. cases
32 ___ vez (again, in Spanish)
34 Preowned
37 Singer McEntire
38 Wheat, barley or beans
40 In ___ of
42 First drug approved to treat AIDS
45 90210, for Beverly Hills
46 Feeling of loss
48 Person obeying a coxswain
49 Significant
51 Four duos
52 Peter of "M"
54 Super stars
56 ___-Tass news agency
58 Court plea, informally
59 Tributary of the Colorado
60 Rent-___ (security person for hire)
61 Wraps (up)
64 Snare
65 Prefix with dermis

by Stella Daily and Bruce Venzke

My Time: _____ min

Beginner: 30 min   Intermediate: 15 min   Expert: 8 min

ACROSS

1 Ooze
5 Neighbor of Kan.
9 Go after
14 Island dance
15 Do perfectly
16 Go online
17 Final notice?
18 Coastal flier
19 Take away little by little
20 Diana Ross musical, with "The"
21 They require signals
23 Neptune's domain
24 ___ carte
25 Number of operas composed by Beethoven
26 Play the slots, e.g.
28 Ohio university whose team is the Golden Flashes
34 Fancy flapjacks
37 Comstock ___
38 Touch with a hanky, say
39 Pro ___ (proportionately)
40 Slacks material
42 Facts and figures
43 Baseball bat wood
44 P P P, in Greek
45 Liechtenstein's language
47 Fibs
50 Stephen of "The Crying Game"
51 Beehive State native
52 Timeline division
54 Carpet fuzz
57 Publication that is the key to this puzzle's theme
62 Conk out
63 Tunesmith's org.
64 "That's a shame"
65 Exec's note
66 Peach pit
67 Treat with grandmotherly love, with "on"
68 Kitchen dial site
69 Sharpened
70 Proofer's mark
71 Takes as one's spouse

DOWN

1 Exhibits
2 Blake of jazz
3 1998 role for Cate Blanchett
4 Butter slice
5 N.B.A.'s Shaquille
6 Egyptian temple site
7 Airport delay?
8 Guinness of stage and screen
9 Make spotless
10 Big buzzer
11 Bug-eyed
12 Slaw, e.g.
13 Hydrocarbon suffixes
21 After the buzzer
22 "Oh, goody!"
27 Air quality grp.
29 Beethoven dedicatee
30 "Smoking or ___?"
31 Genesis duo
32 "Ciao!"
33 Israel's Abba
34 Sticking point?
35 Too hasty
36 Haul, slangily
41 ___ polloi
42 Rap's Dr. ___
44 Entered again
46 Part of Q.E.D.
48 New Orleans school
49 Hundred on the Hill
53 Bowling alley button
55 Pointed
56 Doers of drudgery
57 Track meet event
58 Regarding
59 Revered one
60 Little shavers
61 Jillions
65 Use a Lawn-Boy, e.g.

by Adam G. Perl

My Time: _____ min

Beginner: 30 min   Intermediate: 15 min   Expert: 8 min

ACROSS

1 Prominent feature of Dracula
6 Reunion group
11 Showman Ziegfeld
14 "Let's Make ___"
15 Search engine name
16 Designer Claiborne
17 It may end up in the gutter
19 In the style of
20 ___ acid (protein component)
21 Schindler of "Schindler's List"
23 Spy's device
26 Sweater style
29 Runs out
32 Slave girl of opera
33 Exploding stars
34 Fuel economy org.
35 City in Italia
39 What 17-, 26-, 50- and 60-Across have in common
43 Pageant accessory
44 Tony Soprano and cohorts, with "the"
45 Cheese hunk
46 One on a pedestal
48 Old timer?
50 Classic breakfast fare
54 Suffix with butyl
55 Reporting to
56 How-to presentations
59 ___ glance
60 Item on a set
66 Fix illegally
67 Disney mermaid
68 Sees red
69 Informal top
70 Center of power
71 Some retired racehorses

DOWN

1 Wonderful, slangily
2 Fuss
3 Partner of improved
4 Big bash
5 ___ to none (long odds)
6 Stellar swan
7 Part of a repair estimate
8 "Got it!"
9 Showman Hurok
10 Went at it alone
11 Cereal morsel
12 Purple hue
13 Country/rock's ___ Mountain Daredevils
18 Nick at ___
22 Tangled, as hair
23 Big tops
24 Lei Day greeting
25 Blacktops, say
27 Surveillance evidence
28 Fact fudger
30 Common union demand
31 Part of a min.
34 Flow back
36 Nostalgic tune
37 Mullally of "Will & Grace"
38 Fred Astaire's sister
40 Bow-toting god
41 Certain plea, for short
42 Of one's ___
47 Skin-related
48 Makes hard
49 "Semper Fi" org.
50 Milk purchase
51 Loosen, in a way
52 Bit of wisdom
53 Parting word
57 Klutzy sorts
58 Dirty reading
61 "___ y plata"
62 Trader ___ (old restaurateur)
63 Rhea relative
64 Like Republican states on an electoral map
65 Braying beast

by C. W. Stewart and J. K. Hummel

My Time: _____ **min**

Beginner: 30 min   Intermediate: 15 min   Expert: 8 min

ACROSS

1 Ashen
5 Decorative molding
9 Yellow shade
14 Gen. Robt. ___
15 "Look both ways before crossing," e.g.
16 Lax
17 In front of a hydrant, say
20 Notice for late ticket-buyers, maybe
21 "Waking ___ Devine" (1998 film)
22 Ignited
23 "Uh-oh"
27 Cool, to a cat
30 They might be near I.C.U.'s
31 Hair removal product
32 Tic-tac-toe loser
33 Atlanta university
36 Fran of "The Nanny"
38 School lady
39 Things hidden in 17-, 23-, 49- and 57-Across
41 Pawn
42 Loch Ness monster, e.g.
44 Dictatorial
45 Umberto who wrote "The Name of the Rose"
46 1998 song by the Goo Goo Dolls that was #1 for 18 weeks
47 Part of m.p.g.
48 Aurora's Greek counterpart
49 Publicists
54 Nafta signatory
55 Opposite of post-
56 Only Super Bowl won by the New York Jets

57 Business sessions that drag
63 Seed-to-be
64 Israel's Abba
65 French seas
66 Mythological reveler
67 Hair line
68 Zebras, to lions

DOWN

1 "Taste that beats the others cold" sloganeer, once
2 Morning waker-upper
3 "Vive ___!"
4 "Horrors!"
5 Directives
6 Father ___ Sarducci, longtime "S.N.L." character
7 Pipe joint
8 Epitome of slipperiness
9 Home of the Casbah
10 Castle defense
11 Ex-hoopster Manute ___
12 Course for a recent émigré: Abbr.
13 King in un palacio
18 Contestant's mail-in
19 The Oscars of magazine publishing
24 ___ Jean (Marilyn Monroe, affectionately)
25 Disrobe
26 Zinger
27 Ding Dongs competitor
28 Board members, for short
29 Looney Tunes pig
33 Maker of introductions

34 ___ Polo
35 Snacks dipped in milk
37 Dusting or taking out the garbage
39 "Yippee!"
40 Lake ___, outlet of the Maumee River
43 Racetrack tout
44 Father
47 Father, e.g.
50 Stab
51 Forty-___
52 Un gato grande
53 Girlish boy
54 Hard on the eyes
57 ___ Lobos
58 TV's Longoria
59 Kook
60 Opposite of "naw"
61 Wall St. hire
62 Little troublemaker

by Peter A. Collins

My Time: _____ min

Beginner: 30 min   Intermediate: 15 min   Expert: 8 min

ACROSS

1 Olympics prize
6 "Zounds!"
10 "In your dreams!"
14 Vega of "Spy Kids" movies
15 Marilyn Monroe facial mark
16 It may be tempted
17 Reminisce about a nice facial outline?
20 "I'll take that as ___"
21 Cartoon villain Badenov
22 Gangsters' gals
23 Ambassador's forte
25 Nada
26 Sidney Poitier title role
27 Reminisce about spring cleaning?
33 "Daggers" look
35 Rap sheet letters
36 Trifling amount
37 Common breakfast fare
40 Tense subject?
43 Brit. record label
44 Catchword of 6-Down
46 Wise up
47 Reminisce about working in a restaurant?
52 Pool tool
53 Messenger ___
54 Starch-yielding palm
57 Santa ___, California city, county or river
60 Not spoken
62 Buddhist sect
63 Reminisce about a pig-out?
66 Census data
67 Jungle menaces

68 Minister's home
69 Physiques, informally
70 Cathedral area
71 Like dessert wines

DOWN

1 Corday's victim
2 Actress Verdugo
3 Like a blue state
4 Give the boot
5 Mild-mannered type
6 Lagasse of the Food Network
7 Big bully
8 "The Sound of Music" setting
9 "___ Rosenkavalier"
10 Be able to meet the expense of
11 Go yachting

12 "___ be a cold day in hell . . ."
13 Honoraria
18 U2 frontman
19 Skip
24 Time in a seat
26 Mark permanently
28 Middling grade
29 Heart chart, for short
30 People rival
31 Wing it?
32 Roll of the dice, maybe
33 Attendee
34 Poor, as an excuse
38 Having the resources
39 Postgraduate study
41 Boxer Laila
42 Department store department

45 Salsa percussion
48 Unlike this answer
49 Waikiki wingding
50 As a precaution
51 Follow, as a suspect
55 Honkers
56 Get-go
57 Kvetching sort
58 Toy block brand
59 Got 100 on
60 'Vette roof option
61 Parts of a drum kit
64 Home for Bulls, but not Bears: Abbr.
65 Like a new recruit

by Deb Amlen

My Time: _____ min

Beginner: 30 min   Intermediate: 15 min   Expert: 8 min

ACROSS

1 Puppies' plaints
5 Cobb of "12 Angry Men"
9 Icy look
14 Oratorio highlight
15 Di or da preceder in a Beatles song
16 Moves like sludge
17 "What ___ Did" (classic children's book with a punny title)
18 ___ Spee (old German warship)
19 Catcher's position
20 Enjoying an outing, of sorts
23 "Gets the red out" sloganeer
24 Italian auto, for short
25 Scientology founder ___ Hubbard
28 For no profit
32 Sister of Marge Simpson
36 Forsaken
38 Get ___ the habit
39 Enjoying an outing, of sorts
42 Homecoming figure, for short
43 Yin's counterpart
44 Checking out
45 Michelin offering
47 Flagston family pet
49 Gin flavoring
51 Edit
56 Enjoying an outing, of sorts
61 Like wild tigers
62 Drought relief
63 Hi Flagston's wife, in the comics
64 Garden plant support
65 One hired by a corp. board
66 McCann of country music
67 Cheated, slangily
68 One of "The Addams Family," informally
69 Comrade in arms

DOWN

1 Comic Smirnoff
2 Tehran denizen
3 Actress ZaSu
4 Greet cordially
5 Paul Bunyan, e.g.
6 River of Spain
7 Mideast airline
8 Port of Israel
9 Treat leniently, with "on"
10 Talkativeness
11 France's Côte d'___
12 Actor Stephen and kin
13 Renaissance family name
21 China's Zhou ___
22 Trolley sound
26 Gymnast Korbut
27 Ad infinitum
29 "The ___ Love" (R.E.M. hit)
30 British W.W. II-era gun
31 Chinatown gang
32 Exchange jabs
33 Former Connecticut governor Grasso
34 Speak well of
35 "I can't blame anyone else"
37 Latvia's capital
40 Fishing line material
41 Georg who wrote "The Philosophy of Right"
46 Trued up
48 Twist badly
50 Everglades wader
52 Home overlooking the sea, maybe
53 How some tuna is packed
54 Dexterity
55 Lamb or Bacon piece
56 ___ browns (diner fare)
57 Analogy part
58 Havana aunts
59 Kind of stand
60 Doesn't dally

by Victor Fleming

My Time: _____ min

Beginner: 40 min   Intermediate: 18 min   Expert: 10 min

ACROSS

1 Gad about
5 Donahue of "Father Knows Best"
11 One learning the ropes
14 ___ Disney
15 Reason out
16 Soccer fan's cry
17 Source of rump roast
19 Messenger ___
20 1977 double-platinum Steely Dan album
21 Bygone Mideast grp.
22 P.M. between Pearson and Clark
24 Charity event, maybe
26 Shared taxi
27 Blockbuster offering
29 Panama and others
32 Hard-hearted
35 ___ McAn shoes
37 Came out with
38 Sweetums
39 Speed-read
42 "Cimarron" studio, 1931
43 Children's tune starter
45 "The Seduction of Joe Tynan" star, 1979
46 Can't deal with
48 Like some oaths or vows
50 Ready to pour
52 "I am six. I am a city child. I live at the Plaza" speaker
54 Sports spots
58 Biopsy, e.g.
60 Purpose
61 Assayer's stuff
62 "The Simpsons" storekeeper
63 Worrisome economic condition

66 Input-jack label
67 Regarding this point, in legalese
68 "Happy Motoring" sloganeer
69 Golf's Se Ri ___
70 Unpaid debt
71 This puzzle's theme

DOWN

1 Dry out, in a way
2 Mystical board
3 Ricardo player
4 Chic, '60s-style
5 Shevardnadze of Georgia
6 King of tragedy
7 Bargain bin abbr.
8 Capone colleague
9 Paycheck fattener
10 Summer TV fare
11 "Sunglasses at Night" singer, 1984
12 Limb bone
13 Steady
18 Shows cowardice
23 Police dept. figs.
25 N.Y.C.'s ___ of the Americas
26 Court anonym
28 Footnote abbr.
30 Love of the Beach Boys
31 Wedding exchange
32 Cartoonist Addams
33 ___-call (automated solicitation)
34 John Candy title role
36 Son of Judah
40 Coffee holder

41 Teachings of Buddha
44 Shoulder muscle, briefly
47 Take off on
49 One of the Mitchells in an old UPN sitcom
51 Custom-create
53 Fab Four name
55 Click or clack
56 Cropped up
57 Toledo title
58 Desktop accessory
59 Capital of Samoa
60 Aqua Velva alternative
64 "Hmm, no fooling!"
65 Former televangelist Haggard

by Allan E. Parrish

My Time: _____ min

Beginner: 40 min   Intermediate: 18 min   Expert: 10 min

ACROSS

1 Snookered
4 Discourse topic
9 Raced the Super G, say
14 Butterfly ___ (sash)
15 Underwater wave generator
16 Vegas request
17 21 in two cards
19 Williams of "Happy Days"
20 "The Lion King" queen
21 Andean tuber
22 Sapphic works
23 Circular seal
25 Happy hour offering, maybe
29 Drinking sprees
31 Ex-G.I.'s grp.
32 "Hurrah!"
33 Dander
34 Fruits de ___ (seafood)
35 Use a ewer
36 C.E.O. protector
41 ___ fixe
42 Ranch moniker
43 Ranch call
44 Annual Scripps event
45 Drum site
46 Gymnast's helper
50 Huge amount, slangily
53 Runway asset
54 Cartoonist Addams
55 ___ Kovic, role for Tom Cruise
57 Machu Picchu dweller
58 Like melted caramel
60 What 17-, 25-, 36- or 50-Across is
62 Citified
63 Initiates, in a cruel way
64 Quick to learn
65 Brit's blade
66 Fishhook attachment
67 Carlos or Felipe

DOWN

1 Pal around (with)
2 Loud, like trumpets
3 Try to reach a talk show, say
4 Sound uttered while shaking the head
5 "28 Flavors" chain, for short
6 Puts into effect
7 Brilliantly colored bird
8 Neighbor of Mo.
9 Follow secretly
10 Seven-time N.L. home run champ
11 Dress shop compliment
12 Funny Philips
13 Iniquity site?
18 1956 Bernstein operetta
22 Means of exit
24 "Primal Fear" star, 1996
26 Recovered from
27 Suffix with aqua
28 Brontë heroine
30 Bowling shoes, often
34 Mel Gibson's "mad" role
35 Airport security request
36 Bee Gees' surname
37 Concert halls
38 Willy Loman player on Broadway
39 Gilpin of "Frasier"
40 Place to brood
45 Comic Boosler
46 Catch some Z's
47 Musical inability
48 Go over the wall, maybe
49 Donald Trump's field
51 Rumormonger's start
52 Item with pedals
56 December air
58 Gloomy guy?
59 ". . . ___ mouse?"
60 Starts of sneezes
61 Fast www link

by Daniel Kantor

My Time: _____ min

Beginner: 40 min   Intermediate: 18 min   Expert: 10 min

ACROSS

1 "___ Eat Cake" (1930s musical)
6 H'wood type
11 Familiar sitcom figure
14 Massey of old movies
15 Embassy figure
16 Stir
17 Guy ready to sing the national anthem?
19 Eggy concoction
20 Meditation goal
21 Making the most of
23 Era ended by Vesuvius?
27 Cold one, so to speak
29 March (through)
30 "If all ___ fails . . ."
31 Author Calvino
33 Kind of acid
35 Churl
36 What shall be first . . . or words that can precede 17-, 23-, 52- and 60-Across
39 Vote against
42 Maker of the game Combat
43 Piece in the game go
45 Pear type
48 Martini's partner
51 European erupter
52 Belonging to a Hudson Valley tribe?
55 Colgate alternative
56 Sinews
59 Janis ___, with the 1975 hit "At Seventeen"
60 Museum exhibit?

64 D.D.E.'s purview in W.W. II
65 Convertible driver's option
66 Cache
67 Div.
68 Christmases
69 Funny Fields

DOWN

1 V.I.P.'s ride
2 Pizazz
3 Unable to hit a pitch?
4 Tangle up
5 Brit's buddy
6 Bleep out
7 Football lineman
8 Mid first-century year
9 Years and years and years
10 "Dang!"
11 Title brother in a 1973 Elton John hit
12 Mr. Gorgeous
13 Little canine
18 Mgr.'s helper
22 Project detail, for short
24 Daft
25 Negri of silent films
26 Reveals, in verse
27 Brief life?
28 J.F.K. guess
32 Baseball's Little Giant
34 "___ a go!"
37 Detriment
38 Suffix with smack
39 Less than wonderful
40 Former Texas governor Richards
41 Vote for

42 Liniment target
44 Takes care of
45 Unidentified planes
46 Recently
47 Court worker, for short
49 Gym class exercises
50 Patisserie employee
53 Bottle ready to be recycled
54 "For every Bird ___": Emily Dickinson
57 "Me neither"
58 ___' Pea
61 Payment pledge
62 Lance ___ (U.S.M.C. rank)
63 Night that "Happy Days" was on: Abbr.

by Victor Fleming

My Time: _____ min

Beginner: 40 min   Intermediate: 18 min   Expert: 10 min

ACROSS

1 Wrong
6 Study hard and fast
10 Daunt
14 Game follow-up
15 Sole
16 Orsk's river
17 Like Green Beret units
18 The triple in a triple play
19 Just beats
20 "The Defiant Ones" co-star, 1958
22 Rocket launcher
23 Many an M.I.T. grad: Abbr.
24 Brillo rival
25 The second Mrs. Michael Corleone
27 Felipe Calderón's land: Abbr.
28 Sony music player introduced in 1984
32 Delineated, with "out"
36 Movie chase scene, e.g.
37 Yo-yo
38 Song from 65-Across that's hidden in 20- and 54-Across and 10- and 35-Down
39 Just beat
40 Hashish source
42 Massages
43 Some socks
44 Would-___ (aspirants)
45 "___: Miami"
46 Cross-referencing word
47 Organ piece
51 Pale hue
54 Cornmeal dish often served with maple syrup

57 Gore Vidal historical novel
58 Langston Hughes poem
59 Back biter?
60 Not discounted
61 Terse denial
62 Trims in Photoshop, e.g.
63 Itinerary data: Abbr.
64 Heroic exploit
65 Hit Broadway musical based on a comic strip

DOWN

1 Glacial ridge
2 Deep pink
3 Hockey no-no
4 Rakish sort
5 Something risky to work on
6 Bleach brand
7 One-sided contests
8 Not backing
9 Field utensils
10 2003 Kentucky Derby winner
11 Andrea Bocelli delivery
12 Microwaves
13 "Lohengrin" role
21 Hand-me-down
26 Quakers in the woods
27 Most are good conductors
28 Boxing Day mo.
29 Prefix with bucks
30 Nailed
31 Beatty and others
32 Easily split mineral
33 Month after Shevat
34 Unwelcome auto noise

35 Vehicles at a petting zoo
36 Part of S.S.S.: Abbr.
38 Grafton's "___ for Noose"
41 2008 Olympics host
42 Razor-sharp
44 1984 gold-medalist marathoner Joan
46 Scoring attempts
47 Show contempt toward
48 Kite's clutcher
49 Six-foot-tall African animal
50 As such
51 Fit for duty
52 Conk out
53 "Superman II" villainess
55 Oklahoma tribe
56 Workout locale, for short

by Jim Page

My Time: _____ min

Beginner: 40 min   Intermediate: 18 min   Expert: 10 min

ACROSS

1 Rivera of the original "Chicago"
6 "Dragnet" force, in brief
10 Org. for which a D.V.M. might work
14 Southwestern sheepherders
15 Mythical king of the Huns
16 Press
17 Unending pain
18 Ayatollah's land
19 N.Y. neighbor
20 With 59-Across, hint to this puzzle's secret
23 Grp. that conducts many tests
24 Honeymoon suite feature
27 Souvenir from a bad trip?
29 Le Figaro article
30 Epigram
32 See 65-Down
33 "Come here often?," e.g.
35 Chewy candy
38 River to the Rhone
41 What to do after completing this puzzle, with four straight lines
44 Children's author Blyton and others
45 Chief. Whitehorse, e.g.
46 Subject of illicit trade
47 Japanese leader of the 1960s
49 "The Gift of the Magi" gift
51 Ample shoe width
52 Promoted
56 Gwen of the original "Chicago"
58 Berlin cry
59 See 20-Across

61 "Yikes!"
63 Like some hands
64 ___ Gay (W.W. II plane)
68 Some votes
69 Cain of "Lois & Clark"
70 China company
71 Secy.
72 Dry
73 Jim-dandy

DOWN

1 Half a dance
2 Keep all to oneself
3 New issue on Wall St.
4 Color faintly
5 Sanctuary
6 Dragon's ___ (early video game)
7 Central courts

8 Alternative if things go wrong
9 Bread for burritos?
10 Order to attack, with "on"
11 Made a killing, say
12 Individually owned apartment
13 Former U.N. chief Kofi
21 Multiple-choice choices
22 Kind of approval
24 Actor Tom of "Amadeus"
25 Bialy flavorer
26 Some court attire
28 Violinist Schneider, informally
31 Curtain puller of film
34 Wrap up by
36 50 degs., maybe

37 Former Swedish P.M. Palme
39 Beau
40 City north of Cologne
42 Any acetate, chemically
43 Pope after John X
48 ___ Foods, Inc.
50 Instruments for drawing angles
52 Animals
53 Spanish skating figures
54 Cain vis-à-vis Abel
55 ___ Lama
57 Freshen
60 Be inclined
62 Post W.W. II pres.
65 With 32-Across, a ball game
66 Response to a joke in an I.M.
67 Rocker ___ Rose

by Patrick Blindauer

My Time: _____ **min**

Beginner: 40 min   Intermediate: 18 min   Expert: 10 min

ACROSS
1 Vacation rental
4 ___ Lama
9 Paintball sound
14 Boo follower
15 "You know . . . it's . . . um . . . like this . . ."
16 Watchmaker since 1848
17 Extension
18 Blindly
20 Possible cause of a swelling
22 Filmmaker Gus Van ___
23 Have as a focus of one's studies
26 Place for steamers
31 Feeling
32 Weekly founded by Walter Annenberg
33 Cool guys
35 "Would ___ to You?" (1985 Eurythmics hit)
36 Club choice
43 Neighbor on the 1980s sitcom "Mama's Family"
44 Footprint or loose thread, perhaps
45 People of Burundi
49 All accounted for
54 Customized
55 Import with a "cavallino rampante" logo
56 "Phooey!"
58 Sen. Hatch
59 Expose, with "on"
65 Totaled
66 Intrigue
67 From Cork, e.g.
68 Pittsburgh-to-Boston dir.
69 Wry faces
70 Boston five
71 What each set of circled letters spells

DOWN
1 Challenges for daredevil motorcyclists
2 Blood lines
3 Actress Rebecca of "Ugly Betty"
4 Ignominy
5 Friend of François
6 Part of a relay
7 Relief reactions
8 Unbroken
9 "In America" novelist Susan
10 Blair, Brown and others, in brief
11 Winner at the Second Battle of Bull Run
12 Bronze ___
13 Bronze
19 Runnin' Rebels of the N.C.A.A.

21 Squares and cubes, e.g.: Abbr.
24 "___ a Putty Tat" (Friz Freleng short)
25 One of the Low Countries: Abbr.
27 Naturalist who appears on the California quarter
28 Vitriol
29 1998 Sarah McLachlan hit
30 Bit for a basket weaver
34 Half a mo
36 Skater Katarina
37 Jolly laugh
38 Sub in a tub
39 Bert who sang "If I Only Had the Nerve"
40 A first for Arabia?
41 Some people have trouble carrying one

42 Gets engaged to, old-style
46 Milk dispensers
47 Trillion: Prefix
48 Language family that includes Finnish and Hungarian
50 Hockey's Bobby
51 Blackened
52 Sister of Albus Dumbledore, in the Harry Potter books
53 Actress Laura
57 Part of a makeshift swing
59 Softhead
60 Med. insurance choice
61 Slip in a pot
62 Loon
63 Baseball's Hodges
64 1940's presidential inits.

by John Farmer

My Time: _____ min

Beginner: 40 min   Intermediate: 18 min   Expert: 10 min

ACROSS

1 Gets one's feet wet?
6 Frizzy do
10 Pop group whose music was the basis of a hit 2001 Broadway musical
14 Hut material
15 A lot of pizzazz?
16 Some socials
17 Rid of vermin
18 French chalk mineral
19 Corporal punishment unit
20 1999 Russell Crowe movie
23 Something to shoot for
25 N.R.C. forerunner
26 Scorecard listing
27 Fielder's cry
29 Potter's need
31 "The racer's edge"
32 Parent's handful
35 ___ Club (retail chain)
36 Cyclotron particle
37 Deplaned, e.g.
41 Nickname for the National Security Agency
46 The Monkees' "___ Believer"
49 Scholarship consideration
50 Popped up
51 "Groovy!"
53 Orch. section
54 QB stats
55 W.W. II encryption device
59 Fretted fiddle
60 Whittle
61 In a pique
64 Last word in an ultimatum
65 Getz of jazz
66 Dispatch boat
67 Black Flag alternative
68 Manhattan, e.g.
69 Reveal one's feelings

DOWN

1 Tobacco buy
2 Suffix with cannon
3 Campus quarters
4 24/7 auction site
5 Shove off
6 San Diego State player
7 Goose bumps cause
8 Depend (on)
9 Last king of the united Sweden and Norway
10 Travel aid
11 Coarse sorts
12 Two- or three-pointer
13 Black key
21 French noodle?
22 Lounge
23 Domino features
24 Red Fort city
28 Cookbook amt.
29 Dress down
30 "Die Frau ___ Schatten" (Strauss opera)
33 Baseball's Johnny, known as the Big Cat
34 Mustachioed Surrealist
38 End of the road, possibly
39 Like some coffee
40 Gymnastics coups
42 E pluribus ___
43 Fraternity founded in 1847 at New York University
44 Walkway
45 Stork's bundle
46 Assuming, hypothetically
47 1975 "Thrilla" city
48 Melodic passages
52 Looked libidinously
53 Public to-do
56 Dojo accessories
57 Asia's ___ Sea
58 Campbell of "Three to Tango"
62 "___ Beso"
63 Mafia figure

by Barry C. Silk

My Time: _____ min

Beginner: 40 min   Intermediate: 18 min   Expert: 10 min

ACROSS

1 "And ___ bed"
5 Personification of desire
9 Some Spanish Surrealist paintings
14 Like some traffic, for short
15 Delete
16 Call off, as in an emergency
17 Not an orig.
18 Field unit
19 Perilous
20 "She's Like the Wind" singer, 1988
23 Understanding
24 C's in shop class?
27 Something detested
30 Ginger ___
31 ___ and Span
34 Square
35 Soul singer Corinne Bailey ___
36 Aster
41 Raiser of Tarzan
42 Half-oz.
43 Part of the Dept. of Homeland Security since 2003
44 Agent, for short
45 Tabby
49 Hadrian's predecessor
51 Musical based on a T. H. White novel
55 Like some days of summer, in song
58 She said "Don't get mad, get everything!"
60 Attention getter
61 Any minute now
62 To say in Spanish?
63 La Città Eterna
64 Superboy's girlfriend
65 Spirited mount
66 Cannon of "Heaven Can Wait"
67 Property attachment

DOWN

1 Michael of R.E.M.
2 "Jeez!"
3 Travis who sang "T-R-O-U-B-L-E"
4 Public relations effort
5 Bettor's option
6 Rise rapidly
7 Willa Cather's "One of ___"
8 Hasenpfeffer, for one
9 Its motto is "Manly deeds, womanly words"
10 Resort island near Majorca
11 Longtime "Hollywood Squares" regular
12 TV planet
13 What a mess!
21 Wayfarer's refuge
22 High spots
25 Cellular biology material
26 "Bye"
28 Rope fibers
29 Mendes or Longoria
31 Stylish
32 Tootler
33 Winter carnival structure
37 On the line
38 Sister magazine of Jet
39 Fighting Tigers' sch.
40 Despite expectations
46 Dermatologist's case
47 Caribbean's ___ Islands
48 Film lover's cable choice
50 Title girl with a gun in a 1989 Aerosmith hit
52 Veranda
53 A high flier may fly in it
54 English drama critic Kenneth
56 Obdurate
57 Sailor hailer
58 Employee cards and such, briefly
59 Dog doc

by Henry Hook

My Time: _____ min

Beginner: 40 min   Intermediate: 18 min   Expert: 10 min

ACROSS
1 Choice of colors
8 Charlotte hoopsters
15 Extreme pains
16 Native New Yorkers
17 Fraternity parties
18 Ankle-to-waist wear
19 Harpist's progression
21 F.B.I. worker: Abbr.
22 Pancho and the Cisco Kid, e.g.
25 Prepare, in a way, as beans
27 Like some treated lawns
28 Launch of 2/20/86
29 Some deer
32 Sugar suffix
33 1960s–1980s Red Sox great, informally
34 Locale of seven C. S. Lewis novels
36 & 38 & 40 Grocery purchase . . . or what can be found in some other Across answers in this puzzle
41 Milk snakes
43 Moo
44 Global financial org.
45 Facts
46 No. before or after a colon
47 Yemen's capital
49 "You're ___ One, Mr. Grinch"
51 Coolest, in rap slang
52 Kwik-E-Mart owner on "The Simpsons"
55 1957 Buddy Holly hit
57 Extreme poverty
59 "Eat your ___!" (mom's order)
63 Tropical woe
64 Fighting words
65 Move quickly (over)
66 Save

DOWN
1 Nuclear power since 1998: Abbr.
2 Turn gray, say
3 Captain's charge
4 Captivate
5 Steering system component
6 Univ. of Maryland athletes
7 Latin infinitive
8 "The Wizard of Oz" scarecrow portrayer
9 "___ by land . . ."
10 Irish exclamation
11 It might be bummed, for short
12 "___, I do believe I failed you" (opening of a 1998 hit)
13 Aftertaste, e.g.
14 Army NCO
20 Turning gray
22 You might get it coming and going
23 Say 2+3=6, e.g.
24 Marcos of the Philippines
26 Days of ___
28 Red leader
30 Driver
31 Summation signs
33 Gridiron stats: Abbr.
34 Point just past 11 on a clock: Abbr.
35 Comparable to a pig
37 Greek salad ingredient
39 Long time
42 Castle fortification
46 Hungarian
47 Nancy's pal, in the comics
48 Sour brew
50 Spooky
51 "___ a Letter to My Love" (Simone Signoret film)
52 Some mil. defenses
53 Like some airline travel periods
54 Wrinkly fruit
56 Actor Montand
58 Gangbanger's gun
60 Dander
61 Follower of "harvard."
62 Back-to-school mo.

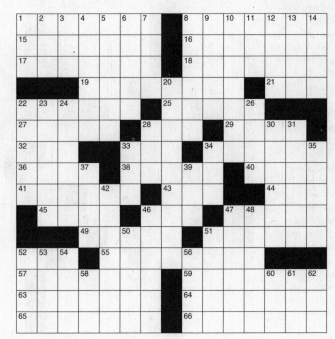

by Peter A. Collins

My Time: _____ min

Beginner: 40 min   Intermediate: 18 min   Expert: 10 min

ACROSS
1 Tub toy
5 Olympics sportscaster Jim
10 Toaster waffle
14 Facetious "I see"
15 Detective Vance
16 Show approval, in a way
17 Salon sound
18 Exec with no ideas?
20 Sentimental sort
22 Like Beethoven's Symphony No. 8
23 Stiff collars
24 Next in line
26 Vast amounts
28 Headhunter posses?
32 Blue blood, for short
33 It begins with "http"
34 Cry of surprise
38 Sweetie
39 Flies off the handle
42 Flapper wrapper
43 Flexible, electrically
45 Hi-___
46 Workers with white hats
48 First rule of lion taming?
51 Starbucks size
53 Tram loads
54 Mrs. Huxtable of 1980s–'90s TV
55 Lacking color
57 Five Pillars faith
61 "Rapunzel" and others?
64 Needing shampoo, say
65 Gaelic tongue
66 Cloud-nine state
67 Driver's headache
68 Marsh growth
69 In-line item
70 Angle (and a three-word hint to this puzzle's theme)

DOWN
1 Part of a jazz combo
2 Shout of dismay
3 "You wish!"
4 Hotdogger's dare
5 Speedometer meas.
6 Groups on risers
7 Ceramist's need
8 One's hands and knees
9 "___-hoo!"
10 Cloud-nine state
11 Quark-binding particle
12 Market upticks
13 Withdraws, with "out"
19 Dandelion, e.g.
21 Streisand title role
25 "Whoops!"
27 .45 or .22
28 "Very funny!"
29 Camaro ___-Z
30 Brie coat
31 Adventurous expedition
35 "Oh, sure!"
36 Cruise stopover
37 "Child's play!"
40 Hopscotch site
41 Sulu player on "Star Trek"
44 Headed up
47 Dismissal, slangily
49 Professor 'iggins
50 "No fooling!"
51 Angry look
52 Bluffer's ploy, maybe
54 "Mask" star, 1985
56 Suffix with Saturn
58 1953 Leslie Caron film
59 Word of woe
60 "Toads cause warts," e.g.
62 Atlanta Braves' longtime network
63 Compass dir.

by Larry Shearer

My Time: _____ **min**

Beginner: 40 min   Intermediate: 18 min   Expert: 10 min

ACROSS

1 *Salad partner
5 Velvety bloomer
10 Dreaded prom night sight
14 River of Tuscany
15 Graff of stage and screen
16 *Takeover
17 Cat's gripper
18 Violin, viola and cello
20 Hitchcock thriller
21 *Pen
22 Half-and-half quantities
23 Mail at contest central
25 *Cote calls
26 Sound from a frying pan
27 Monastery title
29 Place brushed by a barber
32 Sprites in bottles?
35 Bad marks
37 Knickers wearer
38 From 1- to 67-Across (starred clues)
41 Some A.L. sluggers
42 Jong who wrote "Sappho's Leap"
43 Woodcutter's tool
44 Many a turban wearer
46 Toll rd.
47 Sleek runway model?
48 *Sleep lab purchases
50 Lawn care tool
54 Sinuous dances
56 *Salon styles
58 Drink to excess
59 Aida and Norma, notably
61 Chicago's Dan ___ Expressway
62 Kind of ladder exemplified by the answers to the seven starred clues

63 Backspace over text
64 Astronomy's ___ cloud
65 Finishes, as cartoon artwork, with "in"
66 Blows off steam
67 *Fanatics

DOWN

1 Paris's ___-Coeur Basilica
2 Sock material
3 Not suitable
4 Buzzer on "This Old House"
5 Last sign
6 Some saxophones
7 Charles Laughton's role in "The Sign of the Cross"
8 Sassy one
9 It's issued by the Nippon Ginko

10 Director's order
11 Summer side dish
12 When the stars come out in Paris
13 Long narrative poem
19 Mail ctr.
24 Joe Jackson's "___ Really Going Out With Him?"
25 Like J.F.K.: Abbr.
27 Dandruff bit
28 Monte ___, highest point in the Pennine Alps
30 Twinge
31 Beat (out)
32 Norms: Abbr.
33 "I didn't think you'd be here . . ."
34 Hotel front person
35 It might be on one's radar

36 Storm drain, e.g.
39 Scraps for Spike
40 Particle accelerator
45 Collectors' collections
47 James and Jackson
49 Airport org.
50 Event in 1940s–1950s headlines
51 Conclusion of "Happy Birthday"
52 Eye-popping canvases
53 They're high in Manhattan
54 "Oh, ___ Love Jesus" (hymn)
55 Apprised of
56 Curriculum part
57 ___ Bator
60 Increase, with "up"

by Elizabeth C. Gorski

My Time: _____ min

Beginner: 40 min   Intermediate: 18 min   Expert: 10 min

ACROSS

1 Pottery fragment
6 Friday player
10 Rooster feature
14 Giblets part
15 Start of a fortuneteller's response
16 Laugh heartily
17 Dress style
18 Pitcher's success
19 Cornell of Cornell University
20 ZIP
23 ___ West (life preserver)
24 ___-de-France
25 ZIP
31 Mai ___
34 Dosage, e.g.
35 Worked the soil
36 Put in
37 Allergy symptom
38 Pink lady ingredient
39 Sitter's headache
40 39, perpetually, to Jack Benny
41 Port in Yemen
43 Noxious emanation
45 Mack of old TV
46 ZIP
48 Director Lee
49 Helpful connections
50 ZIP
59 Yearn
60 Ear-related
61 ___ lunch
62 Part of WATS
63 Onetime sister magazine of Penthouse
64 Gunpowder component
65 Stationery store buy
66 Martin of the Rat Pack
67 Mother's aunt, e.g.

DOWN

1 Verbal assault
2 Hawaiian port
3 Tel ___
4 ___ Coty, Charles de Gaulle's predecessor
5 "Get real!"
6 Hoped
7 Actor Morales
8 Lux. neighbor
9 '60s hairdo
10 Crinkly fabric
11 Exude
12 Colt carrier?
13 Wire nail
21 Mr. Republican
22 Runners carry it
25 Purity unit
26 Publicist's concern
27 Was a buttinsky
28 "Boy, am I dumb!"
29 Safari sighting
30 It's charged
31 Anklebones
32 Rhett's last words
33 Entry need, maybe
38 Attain
39 Dickensian epithet
41 Cornerstone word
42 Boxer's diet
43 Make whole
44 "Fini!"
47 Pellagra preventer
48 Special Forces unit
50 "I kid you not" speaker
51 Big plot
52 Moon of Saturn
53 "Don't look ___!"
54 1492 vessel
55 Render useless
56 Blues singer James
57 Editor's mark
58 Like some losers

by Nancy Kavanaugh

My Time: _____ min

Beginner: ___ min   Intermediate: 25 min   Expert: 12 min

ACROSS

1 Exorcism, e.g.
5 Certain aerophone
9 Circle
14 Like some histories
15 Addition
16 Toots
17 Scolding
19 Chevy offering
20 Cry from Santa
22 Debate side
23 A.A.A. part: Abbr.
24 You can hear it coming and going
28 Father
31 Paris's Palais ___ Congrès
34 Renounce allegiance
36 Scala of "The Guns of Navarone"
37 How experts work
38 Sporadic
41 Wire measures
42 Not long or short: Abbr.
43 Extremely
44 "Is that ___?"
45 Bordeaux variety
47 Longtime Mideast leader
48 Shot, informally
50 Verb in a question from Juliet
52 Some theater
59 Discharges
60 Not allowing for compromise
61 Duel measures
62 Corner
63 ___ Wintour, real-life editor on whom "The Devil Wears Prada" is based
64 War locale, broadly
65 Company leaders: Abbr.
66 Hubbub

DOWN

1 Old newspaper section
2 It's about 200 miles south of Georgia
3 Anti-rash agent
4 Nevada city
5 Insurance seeker, frequently
6 Circus
7 Come ___ (proposition)
8 Austrian painter Schiele
9 Dense
10 Hauls in
11 Locked up
12 Product with earbuds
13 Literary monogram
18 Classic Chevy offering
21 Wine order
24 Pipe tobacco has it
25 "What Is to Be Done?" pamphleteer, 1901
26 Center of power
27 University of Arkansas team, informally
29 Disco-era suffix
30 "What's the ___?"
32 "I Still See ___" ("Paint Your Wagon" song)
33 Ecclesiastical council
35 Grow impatient with
37 All-___ (G-rated)
39 Nancy Drew's guy
40 Personification
45 Greek peak
46 Place to start a test-drive
49 Quite a bit
51 Chisels
52 Title poet in a 1957 biopic
53 Ballpark figures
54 Modern writing
55 Genetic strands
56 Custom
57 MCI and others
58 One of 57-Down, in English
59 Govt. org. with a flower in its logo

by Joe Krozel

My Time: _____ min

Beginner: ___ min   Intermediate: 25 min   Expert: 12 min

ACROSS

1 Solicits in bulk
6 Flings
10 Commodious craft
14 Detail in a Georgia O'Keeffe painting
15 Plat book unit
16 "Gotta run!"
17 "Lincoln Heights" actress Hubbard
18 Set down
19 James who sang the ballad "At Last"
20 End of some addresses
23 It may go in a lock
24 Shade of blue
25 "Getting to ___" (best seller about negotiating)
26 Zogby poll partner
29 Gave another hand
32 One way to get a witness
35 Setting for the setting of el sol
39 End of some addresses
42 Rolled the dice
43 Renaissance Faire entertainer
44 Some widows
47 "___ Wednesday" (Jane Fonda film)
48 ___ Journal (legal periodical)
51 It's "just a number"
52 Small hit
55 End of some addresses
61 Device for rotating one's tires?
62 Unbelievable
63 Adversary
64 Fire
65 Darling
66 Auto in a Beach Boys song
67 Exchange words?
68 Curling targets
69 "Gotta run!"

DOWN

1 ___ sheet
2 Jacopo ___, composer of the earliest surviving opera
3 Squabbling
4 "Miracle on 34th Street" name
5 Engage in a bit of swordplay
6 Chipotle, e.g.
7 "___ in gloves catches no mice"
8 The Dolphins retired his #12
9 "Oh! Carol" singer, 1959
10 Provided unbeatable service?
11 Swank
12 Douglas or Smith of the W.N.B.A.
13 Afternoon fare
21 Timeworn
22 Hose
26 Not mint
27 Powerful feline
28 Construction beam
30 "Timecop" star Van ___
31 Item packed by a mountain climber
33 Baker's dozen, maybe
34 One singing "Those Were the Days"?
36 "CSI" woman
37 Feds
38 Slithery
40 Hoops bloopers
41 "To wrap up . . ."
45 Exclamation at an epiphany
46 "Justine" novelist
48 Riveted
49 Like a sidebar
50 Runner-up to Ike
53 "Darn!"
54 Kith and kin
56 Prizefighting prize
57 Blackthorn fruit
58 Jazz singer Anderson
59 Grant for a filmmaker?
60 Plimpton portrayer in "Paper Lion"

by John Farmer

My Time: _____ min

Beginner: ___ min   Intermediate: 25 min   Expert: 12 min

ACROSS

1 Ditsy
5 Oast
9 Lynyrd Skynyrd's "Am I ___"
14 Oviedo stew
15 Nautilus captain
16 Allergic explosion
17 Explanation of this puzzle's theme . . .
20 Single-reed instrument
21 Isolated French places
22 American or Delta route
23 Scharnhorst admiral of W.W. I
24 Adolescent outbreak
25 . . . including this . . .
32 Director of the budget who became U.S. vice president
33 Niggling criticism
34 Rapper MC ___
35 Enoch's great-great-grandfather
36 Sticks turned over a fire
38 More than half
39 Anecdotal collection
40 One may be rolled
41 Macintosh accessory
42 . . . still more . . .
47 "Sovereign"
48 Vessel for a florist
49 Busyness
52 Alternative to a Trac II
53 Appendage
56 . . . and, finally, the end of the explanation
59 Rent again
60 Corleone portrayer
61 Aid in crime
62 Offensive emanations
63 Ornamental stone
64 Transmitter of cold war news

DOWN

1 Discharges
2 An inventor's middle name
3 Flaunt, say, as muscles
4 Tobacco smoke component
5 On which an arabesque is performed
6 Varnished surface, sometimes
7 Experts at CPR
8 Neither's partner
9 Lady from south of the border
10 Orangish tones
11 "Saint Joan" playwright
12 Insignificant amount
13 Not just casually interested
18 "Yowzer!"
19 You can see them at marinas
23 Sinatra tune "___ Funny That Way"
24 Access for a collier
25 Inspirations
26 Norse goddess married to Balder
27 Time to close a bar, maybe
28 "I" and "M" in I. M. Pei: Abbr.
29 They chase flies
30 Hermann who wrote "Steppenwolf"
31 Exit's opposite
36 Shindig of sorts
37 Peel
38 Minute bit
41 Monument Valley sights
43 Espoused of Ahasuerus, in the Bible
44 Fish orders
45 Tube watcher's food holder
46 Language organ
49 Beginning for metric
50 Utilized
51 Site of July 1944 fighting
52 Arrive ___ agreement
53 Actress Jessica
54 Regrets
55 "Miracle" team of 1969
57 No lieutenant yet: Abbr.
58 Cool ___

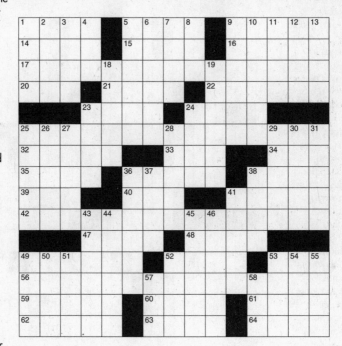

by Peter A. Collins

My Time: _____ min

Beginner: ___ min   Intermediate: 25 min   Expert: 12 min

ACROSS

1 Palms (off on)
5 Egyptian symbols of royalty
9 Casino equipment
14 "___ the Agent" (old comic strip)
15 Place
16 "If ___ you . . ."
17 Certain marine biologist's test?
19 Gainsay
20 ___ Kooser, former U.S. poet laureate
21 Cultural stuff
22 Tops
23 One way to get into a gang's headquarters?
26 Splits
28 F.D.R. agcy.
29 Wrinkly fruit
30 "Breaker Morant" people
32 Lived
35 Eskimos in an igloo?
39 Many a person on the U.S.S. Enterprise: Abbr.
40 Stomach contents
41 " 'Starts With F' for a thousand, ___"
42 Cartoon pooch
43 Prepare trout, in a way
45 Pictures of Slinkys?
51 Part of A.S.A.P.
52 Prefix with -phile
53 ___ canto
56 Wombs
57 Witches' pots, pans, etc.?
59 Cling Plus brand
60 Novelist Seton
61 Kiss in Kensington
62 "___ we all?"

63 Zest
64 1910s heavyweight champ ___ Willard

DOWN

1 "Is that a ___?"
2 Poulenc's "Sonata for ___ and Piano"
3 Coos and hoots
4 Triton's realm
5 Red lights and flares
6 Musical interval
7 ___ pudding (British dish)
8 Arithmetic exercise
9 Beef cut
10 Hebdomadally
11 Five-time Horse of the Year, 1960–64
12 Verdi aria
13 "What ___ thou?" (biblical query)
18 Word with bus or memory
22 Dried coconut meat
24 Poet who wrote "At night there is no such thing as an ugly woman"
25 Windblown deposit
26 Time-honored name
27 Expressionist Schiele
30 Thin pancakes
31 Let pass
32 Poisonous flower
33 Western Hemisphere abbr.
34 Hot
36 Utmost distance from the eye at which an image is clear
37 Triton's realm
38 Not be resolved

43 Kind of gland
44 Like most adages: Abbr.
45 ___ finalis (purpose, in law)
46 Massive, very hot celestial orb
47 French frigate that carried the Statue of Liberty to the U.S.
48 Nautical acronym
49 Who has won an Oscar for Best Actor three times
50 "Fiddler on the Roof" role
54 Carrier of a bow and arrows
55 Stamina
57 Climax
58 Financial paper: Abbr.

by Jim Leeds

My Time: _____ min

Beginner: __ min   Intermediate: 25 min   Expert: 12 min

ACROSS

1 Having surmounted
5 Semicircular room
9 Poor box contents
13 Pleasure seeker
14 Respectable
15 Obtain
16 Ad icon since 1914
19 Acupressure technique
20 Tree sacred to Druids
22 Regular at Kelsey's Bar, on TV
25 Crow's nest?
28 Rebel yell
29 One may hold the mayo
32 Mend
33 "Hurry!"
34 It could easily go up
36 Candied side dish
37 Oswald Cobblepot's nom de crime
38 Boxer's hand
41 Prig
43 Backsplash component
44 "The Female Eunuch" author
46 Bach's "Partita No. 6 __ Minor"
47 Cézanne colleague
48 Recipient of a 1937 wooden Oscar
50 Contains
51 __ Paradise, protagonist of "On the Road"
52 Impatient
56 What 16- and 37-Across and 11- and 24-Down were all known to do
62 Antler feature

63 Roast setting
64 Big __ Conference
65 Reason to say "Now what do we do?"
66 Being, to Brutus
67 First batter to hit a home run against every Major League Baseball team

DOWN

1 Half a huge cost?
2 Unduly
3 Lord's Prayer start
4 Place to pick up a puppy
5 Musical with the song "Easy Street"
6 Arno city
7 Ignore the lyrics?
8 Sniggler's take
9 Bol. neighbor
10 Ring around the collar?
11 Caretaker for the Banks household
12 Ill will
17 Allegheny + Monongahela
18 Famous nine-year-old king
21 Itty-bitty
22 Vacationing
23 Tabula description
24 Churchill predecessor
26 Have coming
27 Fraternity chapter
29 Bottled spirit
30 Element whose name roughly means "lazy"
31 Do something else with

34 Charge
35 Undo a lead
37 Untarnished
39 Out of harm's way
40 Moistens
42 Half a huge cost?
43 Dishevels
44 Literary monogram
45 Isn't stoic
47 Grimace
49 Passing obstruction?
50 Silver, for one
53 Art class figure
54 Opening day?
55 Everglades denizen
57 Genetics abbr.
58 __ U.S. Pat. Off.
59 Seven-faced doctor of film
60 Ninny
61 RR bldg.

by Henry Hook

My Time: _____ min

Beginner: __ min   Intermediate: 25 min   Expert: 12 min

ACROSS

1 Country store?
6 Wrench (from)
10 Jeanne ___
14 Father, Son and Holy Ghost
15 Feminine suffix
16 Even, to Yves
17 Constructing things
19 Don't
20 Couples cruise vessel?
21 '50s two-seaters
23 Custom
25 Some flames
30 Piccadilly Circus statue
31 Annoyance, in British slang
32 Streamlined
34 Cheer start
37 Theme of this puzzle, as hinted at by 17-, 23-, 45- and 59-Across
40 Hard-rock filler
41 Sikorsky and Stravinsky
42 Citizen of Shiraz
43 Hosiery hue
44 Stripped
45 1962 #1 hit by the Shirelles
51 Stands ready for
52 It's made up of columns
58 Part of a camp schedule
59 Means of remote monitoring
61 Hang ___
62 "... ___ saw Elba"
63 Slanted
64 Org.
65 Nature
66 With 46-Down, Ohio State's ___ Memorial Stadium

DOWN

1 Mailing label abbr.
2 String ___
3 Director Wertmuller
4 Old cross
5 Dates
6 Prefix with fluoride
7 Edible mushroom
8 In whatever quantity
9 Museum specialist
10 Ranch wear
11 Outdoor market
12 Corp. budget item
13 Like some calls
18 Snitch
22 Burglarized
24 Oglers' looks
25 Californian's vacation destination, maybe
26 Sources of hurt feelings
27 Turkish title
28 Spigot site
29 Lobby
32 Rub, rub, rub
33 Choreographer Lubovitch
34 Get into some hot water?
35 Actress Skye
36 Start of many an accident
38 Departures
39 Burlesque show wear
43 Subject of a 1940 biopic starring Spencer Tracy
45 It was split into two parts by the 1899 Treaty of Berlin
46 See 66-Across
47 Stays
48 Charles ___, "Gaslight" star, 1944
49 Footnote abbr.
50 House call?
53 Key of Pachelbel's Canon: Abbr.
54 Townshend of the Who
55 Actress Meyers and others
56 Square dance partners
57 City near Padua
60 Anti anti

by Elizabeth C. Gorski

My Time: _____ min

Beginner: ___ min   Intermediate: 25 min   Expert: 12 min

ACROSS

1 Learns
8 1958 sci-fi classic starring Steve McQueen
15 Jose Cuervo, for one
16 ---
17 Director Ivan
18 Most monstrous
19 Taylor, Wilson or Harding
20 Rear-___
22 Book in the Book of Mormon
23 "That's all I ___"
24 Rice dish
27 Place for a houseplant
30 Column of boxes on a questionnaire
31 Defendants, legally
34 Prize
37 ---
39 Supporters of the arts
40 Plague
41 Brute
42 ---
43 Altoids holder
44 Saint of dancers
46 Once, in old times
47 Letters before gimels
48 "The Guiding Light" airer
50 Very
53 Jazz's Peterson
55 It may be said while crossing the fingers
58 1984 film with the tagline "It's 4 a.m., do you know where your car is?"
61 A deadly sin
63 Of tremendous fervor
64 ---
65 Holiday meals
66 Bun toppers

DOWN

1 Pivoting razor
2 Existed
3 ¹⁄₆₄ of a checkerboard, maybe: Abbr.
4 So last year
5 Country singer with the 1997 triple platinum hit "How Do I Live"
6 Fill in the ___ (a hint to this puzzle's theme)
7 Ocean liner?
8 "Oy, vey!" cause
9 Show of affection
10 Film developing order: Abbr.
11 Give a rundown
12 It may be on a property
13 Bone: It.
14 Red and black, perhaps
21 Flexible blade
23 Startle
25 Classic camera
26 Org.
27 Parade honoree, briefly
28 Tabriz native
29 Admit
30 '04, '08 and others
31 Not so well done
32 Hwy. planners
33 Explanatory phrase
35 Dry white
36 Dark
38 St. ___ (common hospital name)
40 Class of '08 in '08, e.g.
42 Ornery sort
45 Risqué beachwear
47 Sauce
48 Venae ___ (major blood vessels)
49 Some fasteners
50 The sun, moon and stars
51 Toolbar heading
52 Boom
54 Famous Mama
55 What each completed pair of theme answers in this puzzle is
56 Frozen drink brand
57 Former first lady
59 "O patria ___" ("Aida" aria)
60 "So . . . ?"
62 Dietary std.

by Matt Ginsberg

My Time: _____ min

Beginner: ___ min   Intermediate: 25 min   Expert: 12 min

ACROSS

1 Locks horns (with)
6 Not Rx
9 Phil who sang "Draft Dodger Rag"
13 *Party game
15 *1961 chart-topper for Ray Charles
17 Stems (from)
18 How trapeze artists perform
19 *Vie for votes
21 Announcement to passengers, for short
22 Taint
23 Rand who asked "Who is John Galt?"
24 Dolly, for one
27 You, to you, or me, to me
29 Baseball stat.
31 Where Wounded Knee is: Abbr.
32 Mrs. Dick Cheney
35 "Mother of all rivers"
37 *Get off to a quick start
40 Corrida chant
41 Hair net
42 Hockey great Jaromir
43 Swell place?
44 Exclusive
48 Star Wars, briefly
49 Fictional C.I.A. unit on "Alias"
51 Calif. setting
54 Escape __
55 *Get it exactly
59 Vein locale
61 Classic Studebaker whose name means "forward" in Italian
62 *Shoot perfectly
63 Words missing from the answers to the eight starred clues
64 The usual amts.
65 Served, as time
66 Gym bag items

DOWN

1 Gets all ditzy
2 Capt. Sparrow, e.g.
3 Zooid
4 Laryngitis symptom
5 Tick off
6 Algerian port in "The Plague"
7 Morgue ID
8 Have as a channel
9 California hometown of the Six Million Dollar Man and the Bionic Woman
10 Selected
11 Stomach acid, to a chemist
12 What's up?
14 Largest of a septet
16 Naturalist Fossey
20 10 Benjamin Franklins
25 Designer Vera
26 Ticker tape letters?
28 *React to gunfire, maybe
30 Chapter's partner
31 *Fail
33 Actor Brynner
34 Johannesburg-to-Nairobi dir.
35 Telephone triad
36 Musician Brian
37 Pleased
38 __ Jeeves of P. G. Wodehouse stones
39 Inappropriate
40 A.M. drinks
43 Mrs. Woody Allen
45 Entertaining
46 Abominate
47 Swirls
49 Targets
50 Carried on, as a trade
52 Bygone potentate
53 Walter who wrote "The Hustler" and "The Color of Money"
56 Shakespeare title starter
57 Straits
58 Doth own
59 "The Dukes of Hazzard" network
60 Unsafe?

by Matt Ginsberg

My Time: _____ min

Beginner: ___ min   Intermediate: 25 min   Expert: 12 min

Note: The circled letters in the answers to the seven starred clues, reading left to right or top to bottom, spell words that can complete familiar phrases that start with "break."

ACROSS

1 Throw
5 It may be found in a cone
9 Homes for mil. planes
13 Object of a manhunt, maybe
14 Score just before winning
15 Skylit courts
16 *Not just stupid
18 Where William the Conqueror died
19 Kerosene
20 N.B.A. center who has pitched for McDonald's, Pepsi and Visa
22 *Setting in Sherlock Holmes's "The Man With the Twisted Lip"
24 The hots
25 Snow ___
26 Les Trois Mousquetaires, e.g.
28 Strain
31 "Eat at ___"
34 Shopaholic's delight
35 Canyon part
36 Daily or weekly, e.g.: Abbr.
37 *Perplexed state
39 1970s polit. cause
40 Early sixth-century year
41 Partner of aids
42 Come clean, with "up"
43 Slippery swimmer
44 "The ___ Report," 1976 best seller
45 Co. with a triangular logo
47 Grill
49 *Informers
54 Seven Sisters grads

57 Major Italian tourist site
58 "Ich ___ dich" (German words of endearment)
59 *Dessert made from a product of a 10-Down
61 Satyric looks
62 Sleeper ___
63 This and that
64 "Finnegans Wake" wife
65 Major rtes.
66 Ivy League school in Philly

DOWN

1 Cellist Casals
2 "That's ___!" (director's cry)
3 "Ditto"
4 Blunders
5 "Well, ___!"
6 ___ Hugo, 1975 Isabelle Adjani role based on a real-life story
7 Through
8 Granatelli of auto racing
9 Bits
10 *Orchard part
11 "Très ___"
12 Did a number
15 Stimulated
17 1890s gold rush city
21 Completely strange
23 Music download source
27 They replaced C rations
29 Pretense
30 Short holiday?
31 Shade of green
32 Garfield's housemate

33 *Fairy tale meanie
34 Put back in
37 Some luau dancers
38 Resort island ESE of Valencia
42 Cigarette box feature
45 Ocean rings
46 "How foolish ___!"
48 Planetary shadow
50 Be in force, as a rule
51 Author Zora ___ Hurston
52 Popular Japanese beer
53 Squelch
54 Milan's Teatro ___ Scala
55 Collateral option
56 Individually
60 Church perch

by Paula Gamache

My Time: _____ min

Beginner: ___ min   Intermediate: 25 min   Expert: 12 min

ACROSS

1 Jet
6 Bush people, for short
9 Retail, e.g.
14 Indo-___
15 It may come after you
16 Spam flavorer
17 *Hairy-leaved plant
19 Many a dance club tune
20 English author Blyton
21 Motor ___
22 Parish V.I.P.
23 Bootblack's need
24 *Fighter at 112 pounds or less
26 Mind
28 "Without a doubt"
29 Not still
31 Seaver once called it home
33 ___ of the earth
37 *Classic comical restaurant complaint
40 Fictional governess
41 S.O.S., in essence
42 Regarding
43 "___ sport"
44 Singer Jacques
45 *Umpire's invocation after a pop-up, perhaps
51 Time period for a C.F.O.
54 Reassuring result on a blood test
55 Mimic
56 Biblical prophet
57 Traditional spy wear
58 *Advice to a careless dresser, maybe
60 Former N.B.A. star Danny
61 Enzyme ending
62 Obtuse
63 Occasion to sing "Dayenu"
64 Gen ___
65 They're found around a neck

DOWN

1 Penny ___
2 Bowl
3 *Unreliable sort
4 Write an ode to
5 Wearer of a half-inch stripe: Abbr.
6 Decorated, on menus
7 Tropical tree-dweller
8 Zing
9 O.R. attire
10 Car discontinued in 2004
11 Bluesman Willie
12 Web-based way to announce a party
13 Gender determiner, as on a chicken farm
18 The same, in a way
22 Third-stringers
24 "___ #1!"
25 Villainous one in "The Lion King"
27 Where punts were spent
29 Bolted down
30 Short
31 Some greens
32 Hotfoot it
33 De bene ___ (legal phrase)
34 Restricted space . . . or a hint to the answers to the six starred clues
35 One and one
36 White Sulphur ___, W. Va.: Abbr.
38 Relieve, as for a break
39 Easily maneuvered, as a boat
43 Lab receptacle
44 ___ cheese
45 They believed the world was created by Viracocha
46 "That's the truth!"
47 Makeshift fan
48 Subject of a certain Google search
49 Subject of union negotiations
50 Caffeine or nicotine
52 Bank's partner
53 Hurls defiance at
56 Assessor
58 Hole-punching tool for a slater
59 Suffix for many a sharable computer file

by Kenneth J. Berniker

My Time: _____ min

Beginner: __ min   Intermediate: 25 min   Expert: 12 min

ACROSS

1 Words ending many riddles
4 __ of Darkness
8 Montmartre : Paris :: Arbat : __
14 __ favor
15 Mind
16 Place for combs
17 On a lounge chair, maybe
19 It's under an eyeglass frame
20 O'Toole of "Cat People"
21 "Shut your mouth!"
22 Brave one
23 Running around
25 Palm reader's reading
28 Furnish
29 "The Canterbury Tales" pilgrim
31 "Well, Did You __?" (Cole Porter song)
32 Uncle __ of "Seinfeld"
34 "Vamoose!"
36 Australian ranch pest
37 Intrinsically
40 "Listen up!"
42 Ending with soft or light
43 Great Leap Forward figure
44 __-eyed
45 There are eight of these before "baby" in Elvis's "A Big Hunk o' Love"
47 Like car radios
49 Bub
51 "Sesame Street" subject
55 Was sympathetic
57 That, to Tomás
58 Exam measurement unit
59 Sat around
61 Fix up for a museum, maybe
63 Revenue worker
65 Jilter
66 Familiarize (oneself)
67 Rise
68 Bastille Day season
69 Changes
70 "Don't change"
71 Piglet's pal

DOWN

1 Dismay
2 Cult figure
3 Like some T-shirt designs
4 Gave up
5 Life lines?
6 Inflammatory ailment
7 Cyanine, e.g.
8 __ Hari
9 Symbol of generosity
10 Fresh as a daisy, e.g.
11 Michael Redgrave war movie, with "The"
12 Magic on a scoreboard?
13 __ Accords, 1998 Israeli-Palestinian agreement
18 Three-time U.S. Open champ
21 Alternative to first-class
24 Depresses
26 Handle
27 Israel's Olmert or Barak
29 Takes in
30 Wet
33 Coast Guard officer: Abbr.
35 General on a menu
37 Asian domestic
38 Author Janowitz
39 Alabama nickname
41 Courted
46 Native-born Israeli
48 Crazies
50 2007 Eddie Murphy comedy
52 It has a big mouth
53 Reached in total
54 Typical lead-in?
56 Middle of the country
58 Genuine
60 Tolkien race
62 __ Stanley Gardner
63 Low digit
64 Fortify
65 Family gathering places

by David J. Kahn

My Time: _____ min

Beginner: ___ min   Intermediate: 25 min   Expert: 12 min

ACROSS
1 Takes off
7 Greek letter
10 Songbird
14 Sighter of the Pacific, 9/25/1513
15 A different you
17 Circa
18 Words before a race
19 Frothy parts of waves
20 Unsophisticates
22 Nice way to say nice
23 Sore spots for athletes
25 Its mascot is a goat
26 6, written out
27 Kind of case
29 Joined
30 Escort's offering
33 Prepare to play, with "up"
34 Help in fighting the flu
37 Disappear
39 Sight just before a touchdown
40 Players in the computer business
41 Some Fortune mag. readers
42 Small sample
43 Can. province
44 Service station?
46 Close
48 Blacken
49 Like some notepaper
53 ___ polloi
54 Even more, at the buffet table
56 Get the gold?
57 Bothersome
59 Kind of particle in physics
61 No idea

62 Put on a pedestal
63 Natural hist. museum attraction
64 Old music collection
65 Certain music collection . . . and this puzzle's theme

DOWN
1 Defeat
2 It's used for wrap-ups, clearly
3 Grade
4 Kicked about
5 It might react negatively
6 Madame
7 Tony N.Y.C. address
8 30-Across cover
9 Little ___

10 Like some wit
11 Bowling lane feature
12 Incite
13 Who "ever loved you more than I," in song
16 News staffers, for short
21 Like some beer at a party
24 1905 Strauss opera
26 High society
28 Keep ___ on
29 Good cat
30 Hotbed of N.C.A.A. basketball
31 Roulette play
32 Meshlike curtain fabric
34 Basketball ___

35 Prefix with center
36 Pharaoh's symbol
38 Began
39 Got wind of
41 Discover usages
44 Bar exercise
45 Stumblebum
46 Turn aside
47 Laurels
48 Relax
50 Free, in France
51 Finished
52 Resolved
54 Cable inits.
55 Thick slice
58 Try
60 Flurry

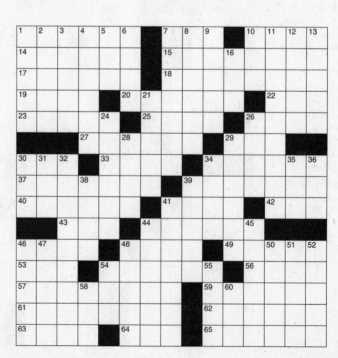

by Joe DiPietro

My Time: _____ min

Beginner: ___ min   Intermediate: 25 min   Expert: 12 min

ACROSS

1 Use kazoos
4 Pool sites
8 Ready for drawing
13 Noted Tokyo-born singer
14 Foofaraw
15 Schindler portrayer
17 Danger from above
19 Typos and such
20 Deleted, briefly
21 Danger on the ground
23 Other than this
24 Euripides drama
25 Go bad
26 Takes care of
28 Normal rhythmical contraction of the heart
31 Doctor-turned-synonymist
34 Longtime "Today" host
35 Its hymn contains the starts to 17-, 21- and 53-Across
39 Creepy one?
40 Humdinger
41 Had a big mouth
43 Makes nervous, with "out"
48 Clever
49 Untold centuries
52 Popular restaurant chain, for short
53 Danger in the ocean
56 Kite flier's aid
57 Lacking, with "of"
58 Slangy motto for 35-Across
60 Raiser of spirits
61 Target of some sprays

62 Morse tap
63 Flood barriers: Var.
64 Address with the ZIP code 10001
65 Holy ones: Abbr.

DOWN

1 Big tricks
2 Working
3 Down in the dumps
4 P.D.Q. in an O.R.
5 Luau food
6 Confuse
7 "Alas"
8 At a future time
9 Soft ball brand
10 Hatcher of "Desperate Housewives"
11 Together
12 They cause jolts to bolts
16 Jaw
18 Has regrets
22 Tetley competitor
24 El Cid foe
27 What to sing while skipping
29 They produce lemons and cherries
30 Besmirch
32 Gravy ingredient
33 General dir. of the St. Lawrence River
35 Still wrapped up
36 Save
37 Prefix with day or night
38 Coffeehouse orders
39 Equilibrium

42 Coffeehouse orders
44 "Oh, no!"
45 Pieces of music
46 Walk, slangily
47 Cheerleader's feat
50 Charles who wrote "Call Me Ishmael"
51 Disadvantaged
54 Plane maneuver
55 Suffix with utter
56 Light on one's feet
59 Guy in Jamaica

by Manny Nosowsky

My Time: _____ min

Beginner: ___ min   Intermediate: 40 min   Expert: 15 min

ACROSS

1 Confectioner's offering
8 Affecting the heart
15 Item in a 1-Across
16 Two-character Mamet play
17 Cause of overreactions?
18 Matching accessory for a slicker
19 Traditional Monday meal in Creole cuisine
21 "Oh! Susanna" closer
22 World Cup highlight
23 Podiatric problem, for some
24 Urges
25 Grand Lodge Convention attendees
26 Big tier?
27 Fair diversion
28 Time off
29 First major-league team to sign Satchel Paige
33 1992 New Hampshire primary winner
35 Intimidate
36 Frequent Styne collaborator
37 Speaks with a pleasing rhythm
38 Bundle up
39 Jimi Hendrix's style
43 Reese's "Legally Blonde" role
44 Synagogue cabinets
45 Timer sound
46 He said "How can anyone govern a nation that has 246 kinds of cheese?"
50 Underground nesters
51 Required reading for 007

52 Offering just the right amount of resistance
53 Wire, at times
54 Give a whirl
55 They hold at least two cups each

DOWN

1 Radar's radio contact on "M*A*S*H"
2 Longtime "What's My Line?" name
3 Brando's "On the Waterfront" co-star
4 First-year men
5 Money replaced by euros
6 Practice
7 Noted English portraitist

8 Beach shop souvenirs
9 Playwright Ayckbourn
10 Frist's successor as majority leader
11 TV host who told viewers "Look that up in your Funk & Wagnalls!"
12 Lying low
13 Montana county seat named for a nonnative creature
14 Hosts' hirees
20 Purpose
26 1982 film and arcade game
27 "I hate it when that happens!"
29 Cocktail party exchanges
30 Board opening?

31 Intellectuals' opposites
32 Site site
33 Had a one-sided conversation with
34 1976 Hall & Oates hit
36 Funny fellow
38 Dog breed whose name literally means "rather low"
39 Wrongs
40 Ocelot, for one
41 Come around
42 Palais Garnier offerings
47 Celebrity who testified at the 2005 Michael Jackson trial
48 Some famous last words
49 Four-legged Hammett character

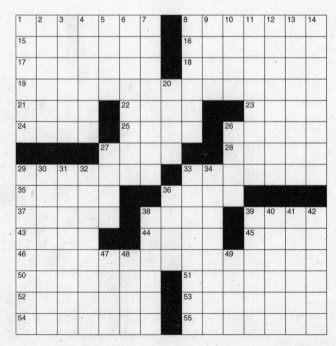

by Patrick Berry

My Time: _____ min

Beginner: ___ min   Intermediate: 40 min   Expert: 15 min

ACROSS

1 Deadlock
8 Watches in astonishment
15 Went for unhesitatingly
16 Luxembourg grand duke in whose name an annual art prize is awarded
17 Tropical spots
18 Plant material used for fuel
19 Brawl-ending cry
20 Beta tester, e.g.
21 Commandment word
22 French city where William the Conqueror is buried
24 Work an aisle, slangily
26 Monk's title
29 Ba preceder
31 "Salome" role
35 Snap out of it
38 Much work to get done
39 Place for good deals
40 Some bridge players
41 Titan's place
42 Blade
43 "Baudolino" novelist
45 It may be kept in a boot
47 Hand tool
50 Unclear
52 Spill the beans
57 Cook first, as pie crust
59 Cardiff Giant or Piltdown man
60 Went through
61 Away
62 University with campuses in New York and Rome
63 Zealots have them

DOWN

1 Sorry situations
2 Gist
3 Guam's ___ Bay
4 Each
5 Bite-the-bullet type
6 Leader of the Alamo siege
7 "The X-Files" subj.
8 Schmoozes
9 Something to bid
10 Dilapidation
11 Gypsy moth target
12 Period of time
13 "Now I see!"
14 See 36-Down
20 Neighbor of Hoboken, N.J.
23 Singer John and others
25 "Fuhgeddaboudit!"
26 Renaissance artist Piero ___ Francesca
27 Relatives of the Missouria
28 Change
30 Without hindrance
32 Steer stopper
33 Sea ___, denizen of the North Pacific
34 Wayne W. ___, author of "Your Erroneous Zones"
35 Tear
36 With 14-Down, something that can have you seeing things
37 Keeping company with
44 Of a durable wood
46 It's seen on the back of a U.S. quarter
47 Some programs, briefly
48 Judge's order
49 Actor ___ Cobb
51 British ends
53 "And so?"
54 Loathsome sort
55 Flow in a coulee
56 Two from sixty-six?
58 Bart, to Maggie
59 Feather ___

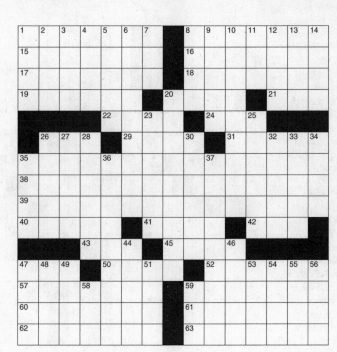

by Manny Nosowsky

My Time: _____ min

Beginner: __ min   Intermediate: 40 min   Expert: 15 min

ACROSS

1 Musical genre that uses a flatted fifth
6 Violin attachments
15 It vibrates during snoring
16 Novel that nobody reads
17 Five-time U.S. presidential candidate
18 Net sales?
19 Multigallon container
21 Grave mound
22 Hostage holder
23 Endearing, as a smile
24 King's successor as S.C.L.C. president
27 Shrink
28 Member of the 500 Home Run Club
29 Cannibal of Anglo-Saxon legend
31 "Science made clear": Cocteau
32 Stole, slangily
33 Sweetums
36 Perseveres
37 You may need it going in
38 Union station?
41 Seven-foot star of a 1960s TV series
43 They may raise some people's spirits
45 Films that require a lot of shooting?
46 Sentence ender
47 Their work stinks
49 What a lack of evidence of forced entry might indicate
51 Send to the front?
53 Unchangeable situation
54 Van ___ ("Jump" band)
55 Orthodox Church council
56 Inception

DOWN

1 Roll
2 Actress who was the voice of Duchess in "The Aristocats"
3 The Pearl of the Danube
4 Sucrose polyester, more familiarly
5 "Travelin' Thru" singer
6 City largely destroyed by the Normandy campaign
7 Literary pal of Tom
8 Witness statement
9 Rain clouds
10 Worked one's wiles on
11 Longtime NBC sports exec
12 "Man of Constant ___" (old folk standard)
13 On the way
14 Stick on the grill
20 One of Ferdinand II's kingdoms
22 House on a hacienda
23 One of the Marsalis brothers
25 "Wild Thing" band, with "the"
26 1946 Literature Nobelist
30 University of North Texas home
32 Product lines?
33 Who's left?
34 Assessment paid only by those who benefit
35 Moving vehicles
36 Without apparent effort
37 Bonus Army member
38 Venomous
39 Cabin addition
40 Heel bone, e.g.
42 Bridge declaration
44 "Politics is the ___ of the imagination": Ian McEwan
47 Oz visitor
48 Supine, possibly
50 Dutch painter Steen
52 "We Know Drama" sloganeer

by Patrick Berry

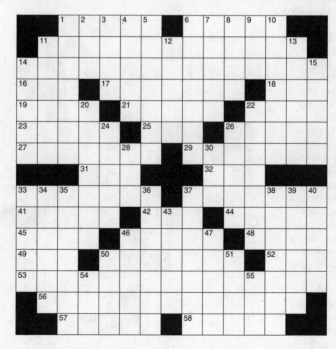

My Time: _____ min

Beginner: ___ min   Intermediate: 40 min   Expert: 15 min

ACROSS

1 Algonquian Indian tribe
6 Went sniggling
11 Singer with the #1 hit "All I Have"
14 Sci-fi character whose name is an anagram of CAROLINA ISLANDS
16 Otoscope user, for short
17 Have quite enough for
18 MedWatch agcy.
19 "I'm ready for the weekend!"
21 Chalon-sur-___, France
22 "The Da Vinci Code" priory
23 "Half ___ . . ."
25 Bygone Ford
26 Place to find a C-note?
27 Climber's support
29 Indian pastries
31 ___ Herbert, TV's Mr. Wizard
32 100 qintars
33 Hands out
37 Constellation between Cygnus and Pisces
41 They're plucked
42 Bird: Prefix
44 Star ___
45 "___ of Six" (Joseph Conrad story collection)
46 "A parlor utensil for subduing the impenitent visitor": Ambrose Bierce
48 1950s British P.M.
49 Mooring site
50 Stuffed with cheese, in Mexican cooking
52 D-Day arena: Abbr.
53 Some licensed practitioners
56 Exercise animal?
57 Hopscotch
58 Tough to dig into, as soil

DOWN

1 Notice
2 Home of many of the 1-Across: Abbr.
3 A long time in Lisbon
4 Fuchsite and alurgite
5 Assuming even that
6 They'll give you the run-around
7 Illuminati
8 Place, e.g.
9 7-in. platters
10 More than exalts
11 Sound of change
12 Mr. Rosewater in Kurt Vonnegut's "God Bless You, Mr. Rosewater"
13 "Butterfly" actress, 1981
14 Clear the way to
15 Some babysitters
20 South Beach, e.g.
22 Northwest tribe
24 2004 Sondheim musical, with "The"
26 Corinthian conclusion
28 Country ___
30 It can fill a yard
33 Elevator button
34 1968 hit whose title is repeated three times with "Oh" and then after "Baby I love you"
35 Make hot
36 Passes effortlessly
37 Miss badly
38 Seaman in a ceremonial honor guard
39 Excise on some out-of-state purchases
40 Mr. abroad
43 Pluck
46 Extra benefits
47 When a football may be hiked
50 Geom. figure
51 "This is disastrous!"
54 Pulitzer category, briefly
55 Red ___ (young amphibian)

by John Farmer

My Time: _____ min

Beginner: ___ min   Intermediate: 40 min   Expert: 15 min

ACROSS

1 Like the reading on a thermometer
7 Molly who wrote "Bushwhacked"
12 Facility
15 Camp sight
16 Relations of Homer?
18 ___ river
19 Service for filmgoers
20 "I almost forgot . . . !"
21 Unwavering
22 Candlemas dessert
23 Private
25 "In a hurry, are we?"
28 Puts down, in a way
29 Forensic indicators of the presence of blood
30 Makes a fraidy-cat (out of)
32 Cause
33 Put two and two together
34 Modern marketing aid
40 Deborah who starred in "Tea and Sympathy"
41 Decorate
42 Give praise
44 Observatory doings
45 Strength of a chemical solution
46 Parts of mountaineering trips
47 Grippers
48 Having the most social anxiety

DOWN

1 Could be
2 Horse of the Year that won the 1949 Preakness and Belmont
3 "___ said many times . . ."
4 Soprano Albanese
5 Put in to start
6 Plant on after a wildfire, say
7 Post-O.R. post
8 Producing some clouds
9 Fit
10 Ones without a chance in the world
11 "Now listen!"
13 London locale of Prada, Dior, Gucci and Giorgio Armani
14 Wits
17 Gets ready for dinner
22 ___ de fraise
24 Olivia de Havilland film of 1949
25 Pilferers from ships and port warehouses
26 Alabaman who wrote the Best Novel of the Century, according to a 1999 Library Journal poll
27 Foreign title meaning "commander"
28 Part of Act IV where Marc Antony resolves to kill Cleopatra
30 "The first network for men" sloganeer, once
31 Overplayed?
35 Claudia ___, 1984 Olympic gold medallist in shot put
36 Tigres del ___, Dominican team that has won the Caribbean World Series 10 times
37 "What have ___?"
38 Fall times: Abbr.
39 Meet away from prying eyes
43 ___-80 (classic computer)

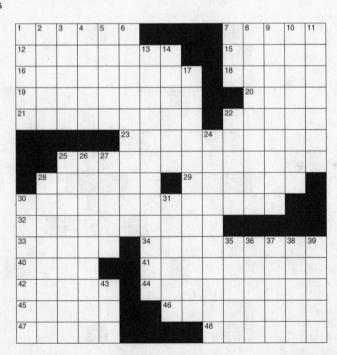

by Raymond C. Young

My Time: _____ min

Beginner: ___ min   Intermediate: 40 min   Expert: 15 min

ACROSS

1 Kind of year
6 Fed up with
13 It can be scary to go under this
14 Key
16 How some ashes are scattered
17 GQ figure
18 Detente
19 Dried out
20 Sound of contempt
21 Indication of feigned fright
22 They act on impulses
24 Like smooth-running engines
26 Black birds
27 Airport uniform abbr.
30 Mathematician famous for his incompleteness theorems
31 Pasta choice
32 One guarded in a soccer game
33 What you take when you do the right thing
36 Co-worker of Dilbert
37 Start of the Boy Scout Oath
38 Innovative chair designer
39 Innovative
40 Natural fluid containers
41 Backyard Jul. 4 event
42 Decision time
44 Fill-in
46 "Bummer"
49 Shortened word on a yellow street sign
50 It follows Shevat

51 "Win some, lose some"
53 Historic capital of Scotland
54 Concerning
55 "Outta sight!"
56 "Outta sight!"
57 ___ Landing (Philadelphia area)

DOWN

1 Pass superficially (over)
2 Free
3 Ditsy waitress player on "Mad About You"
4 Rough estimate
5 "Guilty," in a Latin legal phrase
6 Exchange of thoughts?
7 Burn up

8 Name of 11 ancient kings
9 Some collars
10 "White Flag" singer, 2003
11 Recovered from
12 Believed
14 Sign
15 Transition to a heliocentric model of the universe, e.g.
19 Late rocker Barrett
22 Auction
23 Draft
25 Nut cracker, perhaps
27 Negative sign
28 Requirement
29 They make connections
30 Fed

31 Sunburn preventer
32 Really take off
34 Winter coat?
35 Moon unit?
40 Minds
41 Drive nuts
42 Some sisters
43 ___ cat
45 Practices zymurgy
46 Toiletry brand introduced in 1977
47 Nail-biter's cry
48 Loud outburst
50 Long
52 Moon unit
53 Bribe

by Mike Nothnagel

My Time: _____ min

Beginner: ___ min   Intermediate: 40 min   Expert: 15 min

ACROSS

1 Drawing power
10 Soigné
14 Suddenly
15 Stereo receiver button
16 Steely Dan hit of 1972
17 Villain in the Book of Esther
18 T formation participant
19 Cunning
21 ___ clue
24 Georgia ___ of "The Mary Tyler Moore Show"
25 Perishable fashion accessory
26 Certain sale item: Abbr.
28 Six-time All-Star third baseman of the 1970s Dodgers
29 Ancient fragrance
30 Molière comedy
33 Canadian equivalent of the Oscar
34 Filled treat
35 Properly filed
37 "Cooking With Astrology" author
38 "Moon Over Parador" star, 1988
40 "Buona ___"
41 You wouldn't sit for a spell in this
42 No-goodnik
43 Suffix with Darwin
44 "Divine" showbiz nickname
46 Motivational cries
49 Classic mystical book by Kahlil Gibran
52 Brood : chicken :: parliament : ___
54 Asian title
55 Gulf of Taranto's locale
58 Echo, e.g., in Greek myth
59 Guided missile sections
60 ___ Atomic Dustbin (English rock band)
61 Have as an appetizer

DOWN

1 Not natural
2 Lengthwise
3 Skate
4 R.F.K. Stadium player, for short
5 ___ Carinae (hypergiant star)
6 Attire
7 Witless
8 Journal with an annual "Breakthrough of the Year" award
9 Where the wild things are?
10 Detective in "The Shanghai Cobra"
11 Pilgrims leave them
12 Not randomly arranged
13 Weigh
15 "The Amazing Race" host Keoghan
20 Thing on a ring
22 Earth, en español
23 Hard-to-break plates
27 18-wheeler
29 "Ode to Broken Things" poet
30 Beach house arrangement, perhaps
31 No longer gloomy
32 Rotary motions
33 Be a big success
34 Beta decay emission, sometimes
36 Subway Series locale, for short
39 Directorial demand
41 Thing with a life of its own?
44 TV star who said "Stop gabbin' and get me some oats!"
45 Prometheus Society alternative
47 Egypt's Mubarak
48 Honeybun
50 Potpie ingredients
51 Top-___ (leading)
53 Secure, in a way
56 & 57 Commercial entreaty

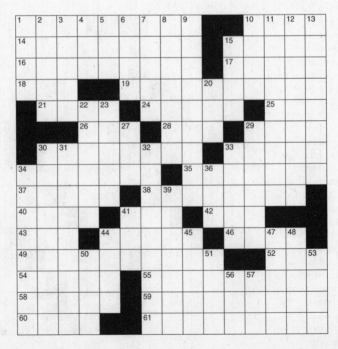

by Trip Payne

My Time: _____ min

Beginner: ___ min   Intermediate: 40 min   Expert: 15 min

ACROSS

1 War-torn Baghdad suburb
9 23-Across and others
15 One and only
16 Weather Channel topic
17 Fleet runner of myth
18 Key that doesn't include 58-Across
19 Up to
20 Ape
22 Habit
23 Shade shade
25 Biblical miracle setting
26 Powerful piece
27 Boarding spot
29 Call from home
31 1936 N.L. leader in slugging percentage
33 Brooklynese pronoun
34 Pilot's place
37 Part of Manhattan's Alphabet City
39 "Be honest"
41 Onetime Serbian capital
42 Show some spunk
44 Drops in a theater
45 Japanese model sold from 1970 to 2006
47 Meccan pilgrim
48 Some speakers
51 Abbr. before a date
53 Underhand?
54 Zip
55 Spotter's confirmation
57 Polit. label
58 It's almost a B, scorewise
60 Pilot's place
62 Apple application
63 Fancy haberdashery item
64 No longer in
65 Judge of films

DOWN

1 Henry Clay or William Jennings Bryan
2 It forbids religious tests for political office
3 Versatile actors may play them
4 Person found in a tree: Abbr.
5 Buck
6 Corinthian alternative
7 It might hold a couch potato's potato
8 Really hoped to get, with "for"
9 It can be drafted
10 ___ bark beetle
11 Stuck
12 11 ½" soldier
13 Online memo
14 Archaeologist David who found the lost Roman city of Kourion
21 Made some waves?
24 Word in some British place names
26 Put out
28 School exercises
30 Zoo de Madrid beasts
32 Shade of blue
34 Enter gently
35 Head of state known to his people as "Dear Leader"
36 "Of course"
38 Exclamations
40 Piehole
43 Swee' Pea's creator
45 Edmond Rostand hero
46 Calm
48 Composed
49 Dirección sailed by Columbus
50 British poet Tate
52 Track-and-field equipment
55 ___ dixit
56 1982 film title role for Bruce Boxleitner
59 Traffic stopper
61 School dept.

by David Quarfoot

My Time: _____ min

Beginner: ___ min   Intermediate: 40 min   Expert: 15 min

ACROSS
1 Temper
8 Ape wrestlers
15 Be negative about
17 Hobbes in "Calvin and Hobbes"
18 Went to a lower level
19 Prefix with 6-Down
20 Body part above la bouche
21 Frames found in frames
22 Clubs: Abbr.
23 Señora's step
24 "A little ___ the mightiest Julius fell": Shak.
25 Actress Kimberly of "Close to Home"
26 Give away
27 Intimate
28 Tahini base
29 Well activity
32 Domesticates
33 Dramatic beginning
34 With 44-Down, Cajun dish with giblets
35 Polynomial components
36 Subject of some conspiracy theories
37 Prez's first name on "The West Wing"
40 Shot near the green
41 Little piggies?
42 Staff note
43 Ad follower
44 Playboy's plea?
45 She's dangerously fascinating
46 They're not easily overturned

49 Stereotypically smarmy sorts
50 Without much wind
51 Tickled the most?

DOWN
1 For one
2 Not at all sunny
3 Fit to be tried?
4 Id output
5 Mordant
6 Suffix with 19-Across
7 Going by
8 Fred of "The Munsters"
9 Hosts
10 Brand in a bathroom
11 Linguist Mario
12 Before being delivered

13 Unfrequented
14 Chief goals?
16 Smart
22 Exclusively
23 British meat pie
25 Actress Gray and others
26 ___-crowd (attendance booster)
27 Make like Pac-Man
28 They're bound to work
29 "Heads up!"
30 It stocks blocks
31 Less lax
32 Prepare for a shower, maybe
34 Foundations, often
36 Aggressively ambitious

37 Basso Hines
38 Hosts
39 "Who ___?"
41 August
42 Belarus's capital
44 See 34-Across
45 Longtime columnist who coined the term "beatnik"
47 Cloverleaf composition: Abbr.
48 Second-century year

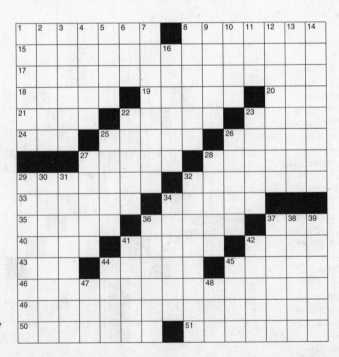

by Doug Peterson

My Time: _____ min

Beginner: ___ min   Intermediate: 40 min   Expert: 15 min

ACROSS

1 Ways to get inside hip joints?
5 Results of compliments
14 Is not misused?
15 Invention convention
16 Bad mark
18 Opening on an environmentalist's agenda?
19 Wrangler rival
20 Pay stub data
22 Person after a lifestyle change, self-descriptively
23 How a goose acts
25 Charge
26 Lug
27 Modern vent outlet?
29 You may pass on these: Abbr.
30 Underachievers are not up to it
31 Old hippie hangout, with "the"
33 "Start doing your job!"
37 Restaurants are full of them
38 Singer Lennon and others
40 ___ shop
43 Where a tongue can be found
44 "No more!"
45 Rolls over, in a way
47 Probably will, circumstances permitting
48 Fragrant resin
49 Cornerback Sanders
51 Torch-lighting skater at the 1998 Winter Olympics
52 Africa's westernmost point
54 Woozy
56 Like some salesmen and preachers
57 Ryan of "Shark"
58 Brushes off
59 Club: Abbr.

DOWN

1 Laugh-producing game popular since 1958
2 What ethylene may be used for
3 Conspiring
4 Longtime Lakers commentator Lantz
5 Kind of resin
6 See stars?
7 Natives of Noble County, Okla.
8 Big ___
9 Short-term relationship
10 Alternate
11 Less apt to learn
12 Much-studied religious writings
13 May TV event
17 Ultra-obedient companions
21 Mugful, maybe
24 Measure that resulted in multilingual labeling on goods
25 They're hard to see through
27 Sect governed by the Universal House of Justice
28 Storyteller's pack
31 Web code
32 Attach
34 They're not positive
35 Turns over
36 Jersey workers
39 Pinch-hit
40 Abstract
41 Have a connection
42 Spare part?
44 Pitch preceder
46 Correct
47 It brings many people to church
49 Duel action?
50 "The Facts of Life" housemother ___ Garrett
53 Silent ___
55 1977 double-platinum album with the hits "Peg" and "Deacon Blues"

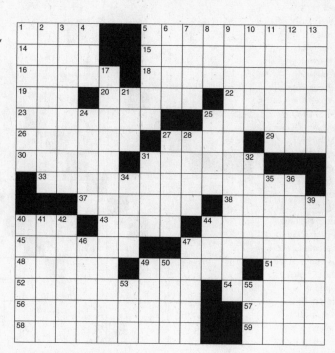

by Mike Nothnagel

My Time: _____ min

Beginner: ___ min   Intermediate: 40 min   Expert: 15 min

ACROSS

1 Didn't take advantage of
9 Muscleheaded
15 He conducted the premiere performances of "Pagliacci" and "La Bohème"
17 Bands of holy men
18 Become one
19 Newspaper column separators
20 ___ Elliot, heroine of Jane Austen's "Persuasion"
21 Star of "Gigi" and "Lili"
22 Put on an unhappy face
23 Revival movement's leader?
24 Strand at the airport, maybe
25 Maker of Coolpix cameras
26 Stray animals don't have them
27 ___ Couple (yearbook voting category)
28 "Field of Dreams" actress Amy
31 1979 #1 hit for Robert John
32 More of the same
33 Like St. Basil's
34 Incite
35 Center
36 Yielding ground
39 Young cowboy in "Lonesome Dove"
40 Ships on the seafloor
41 Roofing choice
42 Compliant
44 Gives up responsibility
45 Sometime soon
47 One with a guitar and shades, stereotypically
48 Bathe in a glow
49 Most mawkish

DOWN

1 Game featuring Blinky, Pinky, Inky and Clyde
2 Photographer/ children's author Alda
3 Jelly seen on buffet tables
4 Kind of protector
5 Pennsylvania's Flagship City
6 Vet, e.g.
7 Stage actress who wrote "Respect for Acting"
8 Pilot light?
9 Treat badly
10 Albee's "Three ___ Women"
11 Vast
12 One that gets depressed during recitals
13 Awaiting burial
14 Files a minority opinion
16 Boxy Toyota product
21 Some emergency cases may be found in them
24 Steely Dan singer Donald
25 Some Degas paintings
26 1939 film taglined "Garbo laughs"
27 First African-born Literature Nobelist
28 "Is There Life Out There" singer
29 Titular mouse in a classic Daniel Keyes novel
30 1600 to 1800, on a boat
31 Big hit
33 Number to the left of a decimal point, maybe
35 Unlikely to rattle or squeak, say
36 Trifling
37 Political extremists
38 Roughly a third of the earth's land surface
40 Carthaginian statesman who opposed war with Rome
41 Rwandan people
43 Blue shade
44 Great literature's opposite
46 Possible work force reducer

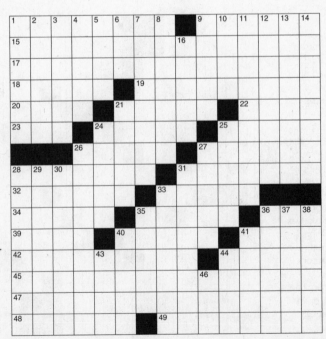

by Patrick Berry

My Time: _____ min

Beginner: ___ min   Intermediate: 40 min   Expert: 15 min

ACROSS

1 Like a Dagwood sandwich
10 Scam targets
14 Kind of flat
16 Hibernia
17 Corresponded to
18 Letter of the law?
19 "Absolutely not!"
20 Treating people: Abbr.
21 Opening run
22 Napoleon's "bravest of the brave"
23 Fine things in Bilbao
26 Feel the same
27 Hit with, as a pickup line
28 Stadium row
29 Cutting evidence
32 1982 title role for Meryl Streep
35 Alaskan Klee ___ (small dog breed)
36 1929 Variety headline
39 Québec's ___ d'Orléans
40 Eye salaciously
41 Club: Abbr.
42 A mile a minute
44 Counselor-___
46 Close call
47 Square dance group, e.g.
48 Some linemen: Abbr.
51 Marisa's "My Cousin Vinny" role
52 Prussian pronoun
53 Ring brothers of the 1930's
55 Adapter designation
56 Enthusiastic snapper
59 It may make you do something foolish
60 Survey of the past
61 Flight data, briefly
62 Charges anew

DOWN

1 Make an unannounced call
2 Floored
3 "The Wizard of Oz" producer
4 "Voice of Israel" author
5 Fluvial plains
6 "Good" cholesterol, briefly
7 Unpleasant thing to invoke
8 Provision in some executives' contracts
9 Some field workers
10 E.P.A. concern
11 Stopping system
12 Stickers
13 Stagecraft?
15 Experts on physiol.
24 What's left, in Lyon
25 "A Confederacy of Dunces" author
26 Not grounded, perhaps
27 Link letters?
29 Like some watches
30 One spotted in an alley
31 Edward VII's queen
33 Radisson rival
34 Carpet fiber
37 Roy Rogers's original surname
38 Rural refusal
43 Remnants
45 If all goes right
47 Yellow shade
48 Medieval stringed instrument
49 It has a bed
50 Some noncoms: Abbr.
52 Acre's land: Abbr.
54 It's plucked in Parma
57 Refrain syllable
58 Crib sheet user

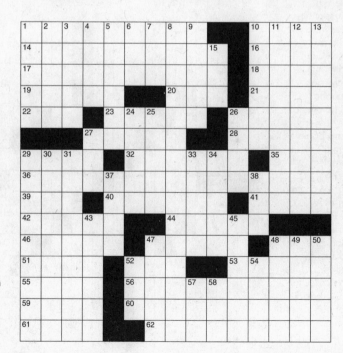

by Jim Page

My Time: _____ **min**

Beginner: ___ min   Intermediate: 40 min   Expert: 15 min

ACROSS

1 Cold ones
9 Kind of kick
15 "Whatever"
16 Crashing bore
17 It may stop the presses
18 National forest in California
19 "O" may open it
20 Product of Berlin
21 Service lights?
22 Department whose capital is Lille
24 Fish, in a way
26 Shell game
27 Formulator of the law of quadratic reciprocity
29 Bergen's bumpkin
31 Horned Frogs' sch.
32 Done up professionally
34 Motor-mouths love them
36 Twelve Oaks neighbor
38 Oppression
39 Brouhaha
43 Title heroine of many Beverly Cleary books
47 "Bambi" character
48 Infect
50 Steps on a scale
51 Are, in Ávila
53 Old PC installation
55 Buttonholes, say
56 1980 John Carpenter chiller
58 Code collection
60 Moo ___ pork
61 "Norma" librettist Felice ___
62 Parrot
64 Alternative to crossing out
65 Camp clothing label
66 Associated with choppers
67 Caught

DOWN

1 Water under the bridge
2 High-tech report
3 Way to await something
4 Terse question
5 Lat. and others, once
6 High marks
7 Tony winner Worth and others
8 Overcasting in order to prevent fraying
9 Where to get bluepoints
10 Okinawa port
11 Pulls the switch?
12 They may put out feelers
13 Take away
14 "The Praise of Folly" author
23 Iron-pumpers' targets
25 Spring's opposite
28 Strike back, e.g.
30 Chopin's "Raindrop" Prelude is in it
33 Perfect 10, perhaps
35 "___ World" ("Sesame Street" segment)
37 French cordial flavoring
39 Obviously embarrassed
40 Like some marine habitats
41 One may let you in
42 Court boundary
44 Low-quality
45 Pennsylvania town connected by bridge to Lambertville, N.J.
46 Nice way to rest
49 Unanimously
52 Make ___ buck
54 Crawls, e.g.
57 Quite qualified to serve
59 W.W. II weapon
63 Loss leader?

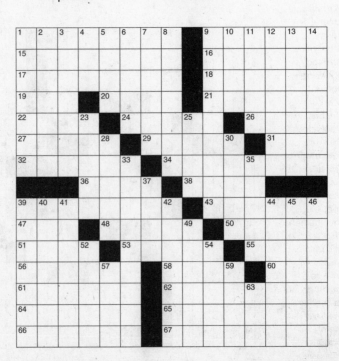

by Myles Callum

My Time: _____ min

Beginner: ___ min   Intermediate: ___ min   Expert: 20 min

ACROSS

1 Choirs' neighbors
6 Lung covering
12 Publicized
14 Phrase of interest
16 Producer of fine threads
17 Source of more pay or more play
18 Baseball Hall-of-Famer Orlando ___
19 Grapevine exhortation
20 Liveliness
21 Veterinarian, at times
22 Stagnant conditions
23 Banes
24 Liliaceous plants
25 Solo, in a way
26 Bananas
28 Webers per square meter
33 "The Daughters of Joshua ___" (1972 Buddy Ebsen film)
35 Southern loaves
37 Pull off
41 He declined a Nobel Prize in Literature
42 One who's getting on
43 Pull in
44 Winner's pride
45 John Deere product
46 Where much info can be found these days
47 Melodious
48 Producers of wall flowers?
49 Most Indians
50 Limestone regions with deep fissures and sinkholes
51 Call-waiting alerts

DOWN

1 Sore spot
2 Something for Santa Claus to bite
3 Gear teeth trouble
4 Prince William, e.g.
5 Maximally mangy
6 Cachet
7 Wolf ___, captain in Jack London's "The Sea-Wolf"
8 Livelong
9 Merger
10 Products of some "mills"
11 Comment of concurrence
13 Comments of annoyance
14 Works with everyday objects
15 Gauge
25 Fawning type
27 Cigarette smoke byproducts
29 Cookout item usually eaten with two hands
30 Nancy's home
31 Direct opposite
32 Dishes out
34 Military wear
36 "The Prophecy of the ___" (Eddic poem)
37 Dualistic deity
38 Skyhook dropper, briefly
39 Stills
40 Receive
41 ___ Gamp, nurse in "Martin Chuzzlewit"
44 Clock sound

by Robert H. Wolfe

My Time: _____ min

Beginner: ___ min   Intermediate: ___ min   Expert: 20 min

ACROSS

1 Second African-American in the Baseball Hall of Fame
11 They feature creatures
15 Some planets may be seen with it
16 "You can stop trying to wake me now!"
17 Simon Legree
18 League heading: Abbr.
19 Linemen next to centers: Abbr.
20 Taj Mahal attractions
21 "My Life on Trial" autobiographer
22 Stat that's better when lower
23 Undivided
24 Pillowcase material
25 Loose overcoat
28 Some home theater systems
30 Fangorn Forest dweller
31 Makeup problem
32 1961 top 10 hit for the Everly Brothers
34 1966 album that's #2 on Rolling Stone's all-time greatest albums list
36 2001 Microsoft debut
39 Web developer?
43 The same beginning?
44 Willingly
45 Melodramatic cry
46 Engine using a stream of compressed air
48 Pay stub?
50 Sequel title starter
51 Gets to work on Time?
52 Spread news of
54 Block buster?
55 Cager Kukoc
56 It appears first in China
58 ___ Sea (shrinking body of water)
59 Lexicographic enlighteners
60 Achiever of many goals
61 It's no longer working

DOWN

1 Sharp workers?
2 Cheaters, to teachers
3 Remove knots from, maybe
4 Water follower, commercially
5 Wearers of four stars: Abbr.
6 Comic Kevin
7 60-Across's real first name
8 Option for DVD viewing
9 Products of wood ashes
10 Flying start?
11 Fan club reading, briefly
12 Either of two father-and-son Dodgers owners
13 Silhouette
14 First-aid equipment
21 When there are lots of errands to run, say
24 "Doctor Faustus" novelist
26 Pacific force, for short
27 Spaces between leaf veins
29 Great move
32 Caesarean being
33 Book before Job: Abbr.
35 Dweeb
36 Conversation piece?
37 Early screenwriter Bernstein
38 Insignificant
40 How some people die
41 Durable athletes
42 Match
45 Many a circular
47 It's worth 8 points in Scrabble
49 Composer Boccherini
52 Mean
53 Northumberland river
56 Creature feature
57 Annuaire listing

by Barry C. Silk

My Time: _____ min

Beginner: ___ min   Intermediate: ___ min   Expert: 20 min

ACROSS

1 They get sore easily
9 6'5" All-Star relief ace with identical first two initials
15 Pretty poor chances
16 Pro's remark
17 Shake
18 1970s–1980s Australian P.M.
19 They're lit
20 Places to make notes
22 ___-Aztecan language
23 Itinerary abbr.
24 Up to snuff
25 Take off
26 Rivals for the folks' attention, maybe
28 Wasn't straight
29 Part of some disguises
30 Org. that fought warrantless wiretapping
31 Words of expectation
33 Raise canines?
35 Meanie
39 Ingredients in a protein shake
43 Part of a French 101 conjugation
44 Get bronze, say
47 Butcher's offering
48 Mother of Hades
49 Dumps
50 "A Chapter on Ears" essayist
51 Where Mt. Tabor is: Abbr.
52 Paris possessive
53 What reindeer do
55 Pro fighter
56 "Enough!"
58 Fail to keep
60 Not at all close to
61 Dessert of chilled fruit and coconut
62 Liszt's "Paganini ___"
63 They're fried

DOWN

1 Filled in for a vacationer, in a way
2 Warned
3 Subject to an assessment?
4 Rushes
5 Fangorn Forest dweller
6 Caseworkers?: Abbr.
7 Muscle named for its shape
8 Didn't proceed forthrightly
9 Flash
10 Jostles
11 Org. with aces and chips
12 Sci-fi author Le Guin
13 Be about to fall
14 Took dead aim, with "in"
21 They come and go
25 Tributary
27 Buddhist teachings
28 Eponymous theater mogul
29 Top piece
32 Grp. with a common purpose
34 "I'm sorry, Dave" speaker of sci-fi
36 "Probably"
37 Gets the job done
38 Catherine I and others
40 ___ Peterson, lead role in "Bells Are Ringing"
41 Beginning with vigor
42 Composer Puccini
44 Certain ball
45 Order to leave
46 1957 RKO purchaser
50 "Symphony in Black" and others
53 Main route
54 Low points
55 "Rent-___"
57 Rx instruction
59 "___ sine scientia nihil est" (old Latin motto)

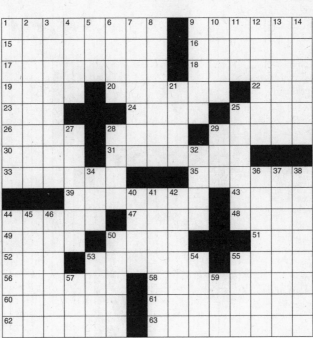

by Rich Norris

My Time: _____ min

Beginner: ___ min   Intermediate: ___ min   Expert: 20 min

ACROSS

1 Lobby, say
9 Where one can retire young?
13 Made further advances?
14 Singles player
15 Lofty pursuit
16 Really moving, musically
17 "The Treachery of Images" painter
18 Whipps candy bar maker
19 Some Tuscans
20 Caret indication
21 Sporting news
22 French teacher
23 Gizmo that measures gas properties
25 Back to back: Fr.
31 Online registration creations
32 Tony-nominated "Pippin" actress
34 Watergate judge
35 San Diego suburb
40 Deck figure
41 Puts down
43 Kind of hero
44 Big herbicide producer
46 Mushroom producers
47 Natural wave catcher
48 Impetuses for some outrageous acts
49 Comparison basis
50 They, in São Paulo
51 Eyeballs

DOWN

1 Perhaps a little too neat
2 "His eyes are ___ fire with weeping": Shak.
3 Creditor's writ
4 One on the way up?
5 Kansas city
6 One
7 Is relaxed
8 Dick Thornburgh's predecessor in the cabinet
9 Worse in quality, slangily
10 Artist who was a founder of the Pre-Raphaelites
11 Encrypted?
12 Stages of space exploration
14 Tom, Dick or Harry
16 Upper parts of piano duets
24 Roadsters
25 Opposite of encourage
26 ___ shorthair (cat breed)
27 Que follower
28 Hostilities
29 Transfers to another vessel, maybe
30 Long-armed redheads
33 Colorado city on the Rio Grande
36 Targets of those catching some rays?
37 Early Palestinian
38 Museum of archaeology display
39 Son of Aphrodite
42 Indication of wonderment
45 Traffic regs., e.g.

by Harvey Estes

My Time: _____ min

Beginner: ___ min   Intermediate: ___ min   Expert: 20 min

ACROSS

1 Modesty preserver, in some films
11 "___ wondrous pitiful": "Othello"
15 Old form of Italian musical drama
16 "___ Nobody" (1983 Chaka Khan hit)
17 Public appearance preparers
18 Introduction to Chinese?
19 Pixar's first feature-length film
20 Finger or toe
22 Mass appeals: Abbr.
23 You may be lost in the middle of it
24 McKinley's first vice president
27 It has a smaller degree of loft than a mashie
28 Cupule's contents
29 Sparkling
30 List in a book's front: Abbr.
31 Like racehorses
32 Spanish city that gave sherry its name
33 ___ Harker, heroine of "Bram Stoker's Dracula"
34 Rocket datum: Abbr.
35 Where to pick up dates?
36 Fall production
37 Rich mine or other source of great wealth
39 Shuffles
40 Margay cousins
41 Siege site
42 Mountain sheep
43 Initiations
47 Graffitists' scrawls
48 Unexpected turn of events, as in a literary work
50 Puts away
51 See-through sheets
52 Banks of note
53 Grant's position in presidential history

DOWN

1 Shell, e.g.
2 Hair-raiser?
3 Bunch
4 Uniform armband
5 You can make light of it
6 Squire
7 Draft picks
8 Private group
9 Even numbers
10 Fliers, e.g.
11 Meditative exercise
12 End-of-year festival
13 "Common Nonsense" author, 2002
14 Insurance Institute for Highway Safety concern
21 Catawampus
23 Scoring units
24 Tries something
25 Mob rule
26 One running for work?
27 Latin land descriptor
29 Joins
32 Scolding wife: Var.
33 Handle incorrectly?
35 Price-manipulating group
36 Retinue
38 Top-of-the-line
39 Rug rat
41 It may be blind
43 Gasconade
44 Name equivalent to Hans or Ivan
45 Tear up
46 Military band
49 Father of Hophni and Phinehas, in the Bible

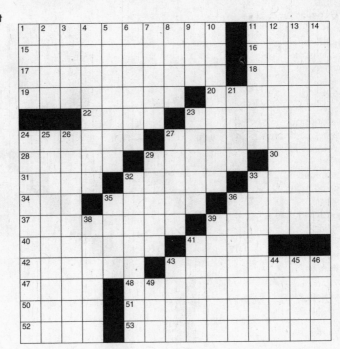

by Bob Klahn

My Time: _____ **min**

Beginner: ___ min   Intermediate: ___ min   Expert: 20 min

ACROSS

1 Saucily titled best-selling diet book
12 Center starter?
15 It's featured in "A Night at the Opera"
16 Tickled user's response
17 Target of a school bully
18 ___-de-four (hemisphere-shaped vault)
19 3,280.84 ft.
20 Suspect's request: Abbr.
21 Internet site graphics
23 Chooses by divine election
25 Ice remover
26 Fig. on a 1970s dollar
27 Enamel strengthener
28 Has confiscated
31 Slip fillers
32 T preceder
33 Alliance
34 College bookstore stock
35 Château ___-Brion (Bordeaux wine)
36 Arizona senator Jon
37 Yes or no follower
38 Abundant sources
39 Lands in the Persian Gulf
41 John of Lancaster
42 Ben Jonson poem
43 N.F.L. salary limit
47 Like 1, but not I
48 Rest
49 Peggy of "The Dukes of Hazzard"

50 Not be generous with
51 They really ought to be kicked
54 Next to nothing?
55 Sign of stress?
56 An alien may take it: Abbr.
57 Is a hero

DOWN

1 University of Alaska Southeast campus site
2 Anne of fashion
3 ___ disco (European dance music)
4 Reactor overseer: Abbr.
5 Cry from a daredevil cyclist

6 1884 short story by Guy de Maupassant
7 St. ___ (Caribbean island, familiarly)
8 Wee, to a wee 'un
9 Foremost
10 Private dos?
11 They're straight
12 Yosemite Valley peak
13 Dumped
14 Harms
22 Manhattan's place
24 Every month has one
25 Ticket
27 Babes
28 Where Fredo Corleone gets shot
29 Passive-aggressive and the like

30 Common desiccant
31 Kentucky college
34 Body found high in the Andes
35 Where to hang, in slang
37 Steinbeck's birthplace
38 Apiece
40 No Yankee fan
41 Light into
43 Governor who helped found Ohio State University
44 Called out
45 UnitedHealth rival
46 Like plaster
48 Suffix with super
52 Explorer, e.g.
53 Dating letters

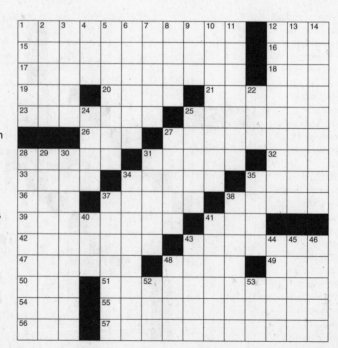

by Paula Gamache

My Time: _____ min

Beginner: ___ min   Intermediate: ___ min   Expert: 20 min

ACROSS

1 Energize
10 Food fight noise
15 "Tom Jones" beat it for Best Picture of 1963
16 Singer Bryson
17 Cocky competitors might take them on
18 Star Steeler Stautner
19 Sends off again
20 Beards
21 Not do anything about
24 Basketmaker?
28 Touristy resort borough SE of Scranton, Pa.
32 Christmas story bad guy
33 Record holder
34 Writer of a five-volume Henry James biography
35 Curling setting
36 Young 'uns
37 Much unscripted fare
39 High hideaway
40 Acquisition before becoming a resident
41 Comparatively close
42 Fits behind the wheel?
44 1984 Cyndi Lauper hit
47 House style
52 Middle Eastern dish
53 Recording session starter
55 Stampless I.R.S. submission
56 Sultana-stuffed treat
57 Exercise
58 Showed

DOWN

1 Plymouth Reliant, for one
2 River at Rennes
3 Frames a collector might frame
4 "Citizen ___" (1992 autobiography)
5 Having turned
6 Monkey
7 Historically significant trial
8 Elementary school trio?
9 Univ. helpers
10 Small trunks
11 Achievement by 30-Down that had been previously unattained
12 Legal scholar Guinier
13 Rose's beau on Broadway
14 Web sites?
20 Take a bit of one's savings, say
22 Place of refinement
23 State second: Abbr.
24 Col. Potter on "M*A*S*H," to pals
25 Turned over
26 Mountain nymph
27 Title sport in a 1975 James Caan film
29 "Laborare est ___" ("to work is to pray")
30 Big name at the 1976 Olympics
31 1987 world figure skating champion
33 Having spokes
35 Leave in difficulty
38 Acknowledgment on a slip
39 Sterile
41 1994 U.S. Open winner
43 Sharp
44 Shoot out
45 Record holder
46 Designer Saab
48 View from Catania
49 Hands are under one: Abbr.
50 Steinbeck figure
51 Title
53 Many workers look forward to it: Abbr.
54 Golfer Woosnam

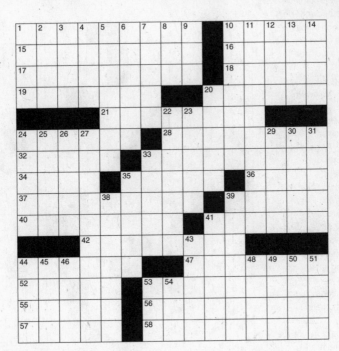

by Frederick J. Healy

My Time: _____ min

Beginner: __ min   Intermediate: __ min   Expert: 20 min

ACROSS

1 Mesoamericans of old
7 Mekong River sights
14 Warm up, as leftovers
15 Freak out
16 Small cavity, as around a cactus spine
17 Embassy issue?
18 Short cut
19 Look at a Playboy Club?
21 1993 rap hit with the repeated lyric "Bow wow wow yippy yo yippy yay"
22 Big name in sportswear
24 Concordat
26 Role in a Tchaikovsky ballet
27 Battlers, at times
29 Fiat headquarters
31 Part of many cultural venue names: Abbr.
32 Shrill
34 Long rides?
36 See 15-Down
40 Rise partly
41 Echelons
43 Gridiron stat: Abbr.
46 "Dead Souls" novelist
48 Platters' platters players
49 Indisposed
51 Gulf of ___, body of water next to Viet Nam
53 Bring down
54 Lit
56 Jim Beam and others
58 Univ. of ___, alma mater of Joe Namath and Bart Starr

59 Infer
61 Higher-priced
63 Put on the line, perhaps
64 Sportscaster with the catchphrase "Oh, my!"
65 Superlatively derogatory
66 Having one's feet up, say

DOWN

1 Mideast expert, maybe
2 Love all
3 Simon & Garfunkel hit after "Mrs. Robinson"
4 Affirmative action letters
5 ___ letters
6 Acclivitous

7 Adolphe with an instrument named after him
8 Not blasé
9 New York City transportation option
10 Hard-top
11 Sharp
12 Certain diet restriction
13 Influential one
15 Noted 36-Across passenger
20 Down
23 Actress Mazar and others
25 Rabbit food?
28 Christmas song favorite since 1949
30 Little terrors
33 Prefix with parasite
35 Letter finisher
37 Water towers?

38 Refuge
39 Father-and-son comedic actors
42 Comparatively bulky
43 Groups of plants
44 Entered
45 What a game plan leads to?
47 Romantic narrative
50 Helped, in a way, with "over"
52 Title role for Maria Callas in her only film
55 Mercury-Atlas 5 rider
57 Turned on
60 When repeated, an old-fashioned cry
62 ___ Lyman & His California Orchestra, popular 1920s–'40s band

by David J. Kahn

My Time: _____ min

Beginner: ___ min   Intermediate: ___ min   Expert: 20 min

ACROSS

1 Cash cache, often
10 No surprise outcomes
15 Happy
16 Liner threat, once
17 Well again
18 Spanish table wine
19 "Isaac's Storm" author Larson
20 Player of the Queen Mother in "The Queen," 2006
21 Determined to execute
22 Wanton type
24 Please, to Pachelbel
26 Shout across the Seine?
27 Green vehicle
29 They don't stay hot for very long
30 It's prohibited by the Telephone Consumer Protection Act of 1991
34 Vitamin A
36 Toughens
37 Kind of party
38 General equivalent
40 "New York City Rhythm" singer
41 Bills
42 "Turandot" composer Ferruccio ___
44 Sr.'s test
45 Dad's rival
46 Iranian filmmaker Kiarostami
51 Weasley family's owl, in Harry Potter books
53 Breaking sticks
55 Minnelli of Broadway
56 Biblical woman who renamed herself Mara
57 What kids might roll down
59 Old lab items akin to Bunsen burners
60 Darkroom equipment
61 Cold weather
62 Blues guitarist Vaughan

DOWN

1 They're seedy
2 Glass work
3 Ibid. relative
4 Crackpot
5 Hip-hop producer Gotti
6 "Vous ___ ici"
7 Peer group setting?
8 Peaked
9 Dwarf, maybe
10 Ill-prepared worker?
11 Drama honor
12 Potential canine saver
13 Personal manager
14 Playwright/painter Wyspianski
23 Direct
25 Mine shaft tool
28 Honeydew alternative
29 The Yasawa Islands are part of it
30 "The Thief's Journal" author
31 Review unfairly, maybe
32 Tops
33 Cheryl's "Charlie's Angels" role
35 Alex portrayer on "Lost"
39 Reels
40 Light white wine
43 Look askance
45 Rapture
47 Eight-time Grammy winner Mary J. ___
48 Patient one
49 Hyundai sedan
50 Fresh
52 It has an exclave on the Strait of Hormuz
54 Pomeranian or Dalmatian
58 Asian honorific

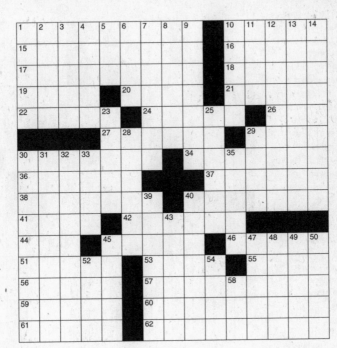

by Karen M. Tracey

My Time: _____ min

Beginner: __ min   Intermediate: __ min   Expert: 20 min

ACROSS

1 "The County Chairman" playwright, 1903
4 Hershey brand
8 Tree
14 Spinners, for short
15 Southern university whose campus is a botanical garden
16 Interstice
17 Having the most pizazz
19 Cap and bells wearer
20 Convict
22 Meter readers?
23 Kind of batting stance
24 Nos.
25 Reddish-brown
26 Al-___
27 Big bang creator
28 Fifth qtrs.
29 Enforce the rules
31 Italian mine
32 Has as a foundation
33 "Rugrats" dad
36 Easter-related
37 "___ now the very witching time of night": Hamlet
38 Norm of "This Old House"
41 Coup d'___ (survey made with a glance)
42 Part of a moonscape
43 No longer under consideration
44 Tetris objectives
45 Like clayware
46 Seemingly silent types
49 Burns
50 "She's gonna blow!"
52 Ferris Bueller's girlfriend
53 Spoils
54 Where the utricle is
55 Like haunted houses, compared to ordinary houses
56 Good-looker
57 The Wildcats of the Big 12 Conf.

DOWN

1 Hoelike cutting tool
2 Neighbor of Somalia
3 Brewed drink
4 Checks
5 Two-time figure-skating Olympic gold medalist Protopopov
6 Snapped
7 Ecstatic
8 Option for wings
9 Smeltery input
10 Paraphrase, say
11 A jiffy
12 Decides
13 Least spotted
18 British P.M. when the U.S. Constitution was signed
21 Quality that's hard to express
22 Event for a king and queen
26 Father of Harmonia
27 Former Giant Robb ___
30 Gymnastics move
32 Butt
33 1979 film with sequels II to VI
34 Prophet of Thebes, struck blind by Athena when he accidentally saw her bathing
35 Drew on
36 Popular dish in an Asian cuisine
38 Guide
39 Zyzzyva, e.g.
40 Malignity
42 Protein-rich paste
44 Certain softball pitch
45 Amendment that prevents being subjected to double jeopardy
47 Oscar-winning French film director ___ Clément
48 Article in Hoy
51 Robert Morse Tony-winning role

by Natan Last

My Time: _____ min

Beginner: ___ min   Intermediate: ___ min   Expert: 20 min

ACROSS

1 It can really bite
8 Warrant
15 See 33-Down
16 Late afternoon, typically
17 Nothingness
18 Temporary
19 Former major-league pitcher ___ Seo
20 Home of Clarke College
22 Plymouth-to-London dir.
23 1847 tale of the South Seas
25 One of the losers in the War of the Pacific
26 Asian bowlful
28 Hot spots
30 Night table
32 Key word
33 Glut
34 Home of Waterloo: Abbr.
35 Growing problem?
38 Pick-up and drop-off point: Abbr.
40 French mathematician Cartan
41 Grain sorghum with stout, leafy stalks
45 Mush
47 It covers six time zones
48 Asked too much?
49 Sport
51 It's pulled by una locomotora
52 Plasma component
53 Foundation with ties
56 Dummy
57 It doesn't help much when it's cold

59 Where Mt. Suribachi is
61 Middle third of a famous motto
62 Puts down
63 Cicero, e.g.
64 Factor

DOWN

1 Latin American capital
2 Founding member of the Justice League
3 Prevent
4 Title robot in an Isaac Asimov short story
5 Lacking interest
6 Basic exercise routine
7 Fence-sitter's answer

8 Post codes?
9 Dish describer
10 Some prayers
11 Taxonomic suffix
12 Electrician
13 Standing out
14 Set right again
21 Built up
24 ___ wonder (athlete known for a single great play)
27 Hanna-Barbera character
29 Agent Gold on HBO's "Entourage"
31 Capo ___ capi (Bologna boss)
33 With 15-Across, sites for some corals
36 Come together
37 Kingston pop

38 Pinchpenny
39 Classic 1934 novel set in Prohibition-era New York City, with "The"
42 The moon has one
43 Madison Avenue types
44 Zipped by
45 Zip providers
46 Clever
47 Yarn variety
50 Bear
54 ". . . outrageous fortune, ___ . . .": Shak.
55 "Paradise Lost" illustrator
58 State with the lowest high point (345 feet): Abbr.
60 "The Gift of the Magi" hero

by Shannon Burns

My Time: _____ min

Beginner: __ min   Intermediate: __ min   Expert: 20 min

ACROSS

1 Bristles
8 Post boxes?
15 Thinner option
16 Piece of silver, say
17 Lab tube
18 A lot of foreign intelligence intercepts
19 Relatively remote
20 Many-sided problems
21 Ready to be put to bed
22 "Rugrats" baby
23 Isn't O.K.
25 One of the Gandhis
26 Golden fish stocked in ornamental pools
27 Christening spot
28 Nottingham's river
29 Dirt
31 One protected by a collie
32 Patron of Paris
35 One making calls
38 Schubert's "Eine Kleine Trauermusik," e.g.
39 Demand
43 Some apéritifs
45 Mother of Hyacinth, in myth
46 Hindu sage
47 Certain alkene
48 Incubator
49 Slew
50 Anti-ship missile that skims waves at nearly the speed of sound
52 Touch-related
53 Part of a special delivery?

54 Be quite enough for
55 Amscray
56 Hamlet, notably
57 Give a bad name
58 "On Your Toes" composer

DOWN

1 "The View," essentially
2 Home to Mount Chimborazo
3 Earthen casserole dish
4 Letting stand
5 Decayed
6 Put in up front
7 Skittish herd
8 Small, deep-fried pork cube
9 C_2H_4
10 Size up
11 Bait
12 Singer of "A Foggy Day" in "A Damsel in Distress"
13 Isn't very visible
14 Shooter that may be digital, for short
22 Caused to be scored, as a run
24 European Union member: Abbr.
26 Means of public protest
30 Was broad on the boards
33 Big Mac request
34 Real
35 Island entertainer
36 Kind of water
37 Nearest, to Nero
40 Lessen
41 One using a crib
42 They work the earth
44 Apply messily
49 __ Nurmi, nine-time track gold medalist in 1920s Olympics
51 Chowderhead
52 Peter or Paul, but not Mary
53 Picture producers

by Tony Orbach

My Time: _____ min

Beginner: ___ min   Intermediate: ___ min   Expert: 20 min

ACROSS
1 Rather good at reporting
4 "Moses" author
8 One given to gushing
14 "Turn to Stone" grp.
15 Dynasty of Confucius
16 Rabbit ears, e.g.
17 College entrance consideration
19 Still in the original package
20 Gets ready beforehand, in a way
21 Like Satan worshipers
22 Lends
23 Past tense?
24 One that gives you an eyeful?
26 Corporeal cord
27 Drain feature
28 Like many churches
30 Years
31 Storied home wrecker
38 Shout to the team
42 Antarctica's ___ Coast
43 Enter quietly
45 Turn (to)
46 Taking off
47 Source of some scars
48 Hierarchs
49 Famous Cremona family
50 Water, in other words
51 Religious exhortation
52 Some injections
53 Coastline feature

54 Current entry points
55 Disposal items
56 Even

DOWN
1 Regardless of
2 Not at all calm
3 Need for taking 9-Down
4 Proper relationship
5 Skyrocket
6 Feature of some roller coasters
7 Rose and burgundy, e.g.
8 Tell a thing or two
9 They may be brought to a business meeting
10 Ritzy
11 Taqueria order

12 "Have mercy" in Masses
13 Pittance
18 Goose-pimply
25 They're baited in rings
29 Tough request
31 Rush in a movie theater
32 Professional light bulb producers?
33 Suppressing opposition brutally
34 Eradicated, with "out"
35 Hop offerer
36 Has trouble standing
37 Architecture, e.g.
38 Skilled moneymaker
39 Whole

40 Certain marble
41 Uncomfortable position
44 Las ___
48 Step, in Seville

by Sherry O. Blackard

The New York Times
CROSSWORDS
SMART PUZZLES PRESENTED WITH STYLE

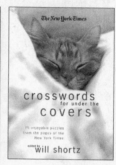
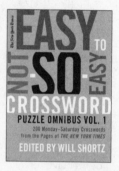

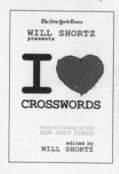

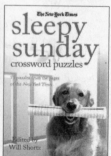

Available at your local bookstore or online at nytimes.com/nytstore.

 St. Martin's Griffin

1

```
ATOM  · ECON   COLAS
LIMO  MOLE     ORALS
ALAN  IAGO     EGRET
STRONGLANGUAGE
      LARS   LORNE
DOTIME   LIN   SPUR
EVITA   RAGES   RTE
MIGHTYAPHRODITE
ONE   HEIST   NINES
BERG   ANE   SARTRE
   WEARS   MITT
   POTENTPOTABLES
ROOST   OLLA   IONA
OLDEN   REAR   KNOW
ZESTA   MARS   EELS
```

2

```
WALSH     KEN   PSST
ATARI   ARCH   ALTO
SPRINGROLL   DIAN
HAG   TOSCA   SUNNY
   ROTATE   IDTAG
      STINGRAY   SPA
ELSA   TAR   MESHES
DOWRY   LEA   STORK
ARISES   GUM   ATMS
MEN   SINGSONG
   GEESE   TRUSTS
DIVAS   SCROD   WPA
AMOS   STRINGBEAN
DATE   PLEA   ERECT
AXED   YEW   DANES
```

3

```
ALMA   IBAR   SIDEB
MUON   RILE   PRADA
SARATOGASPRINGS
OUTLANDS   RASCAL
   GOTO   NOWHERE
NIAGARAFALLS
ORG   RELINE   ESAU
MEETS   TET   SAILS
ESSO   TERESA   LAP
   LARRYSUMMERS
CAMERAS   LOAN
ADORES   ATLANTIS
JONATHANWINTERS
USONE   OKIE   ARAT
NESTS   LAGS   SANS
```

4

```
JAMBS   IMPEI   BOX
AWAIT   NAILS   OHM
PARTYANIMAL   RIA
ARISEN   TEL   ANON
NEO   DEAN   HST
   CREDITREPORT
RAPPERS   OER   REO
ACROSS   SEGUES
ITO   HES   ATTENDS
LIFEINPRISON
   ESP   LOTT   PDA
LOST   PIC   OSIRIS
IRS   PICKUPTRUCK
NCO   ATEIN   DONEE
EAR   WARNS   SNERD
```

5

```
SCADS   VAST   BLEW
KOREA   ARIA   LEAH
IRONFILING   ONCE
DAM   ENID   SOOTHE
SLANTED   LAUD
      AIR   SPLITSUP
THEMET   AGE   YORE
HEXES   CIA   SPLAT
ERIC   CON   SPIELS
NOTAWHIT   WIN
   LOON   CARGOES
ANGLER   COMA   MRI
BALI   TOPBILLING
EDEN   LIAR   EATIN
TANG   ELSA   DOSES
```

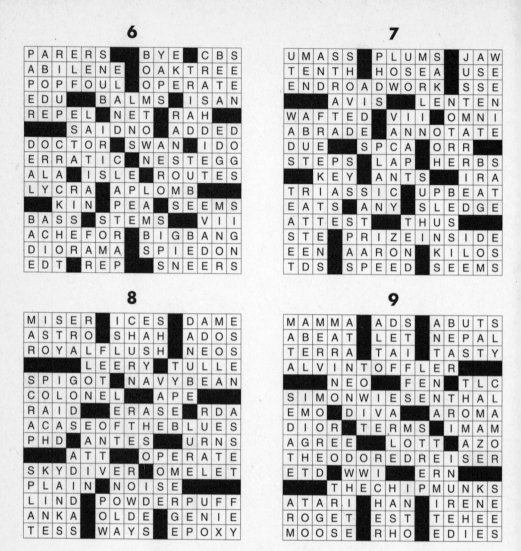

6

```
P A R E R S   B Y E   C B S
A B I L E N E   O A K T R E E
P O P F O U L   O P E R A T E
E D U   B A L M S   I S A N
R E P E L   N E T   R A H
    S A I D N O   A D D E D
D O C T O R   S W A N   I D O
E R R A T I C   N E S T E G G
A L A   I S L E   R O U T E S
L Y C R A   A P L O M B
  K I N   P E A   S E E M S
B A S S   S T E M S   V I I
A C H E F O R   B I G B A N G
D I O R A M A   S P I E D O N
E D T   R E P   S N E E R S
```

7

```
U M A S S   P L U M S   J A W
T E N T H   H O S E A   U S E
E N D R O A D W O R K   S S E
    A V I S   L E N T E N
W A F T E D   V I I   O M N I
A B R A D E   A N N O T A T E
D U E   S P C A   O R R
S T E P S   L A P   H E R B S
  K E Y   A N T S   I R A
T R I A S S I C   U P B E A T
E A T S   A N Y   S L E D G E
A T T E S T   T H U S
S T E   P R I Z E I N S I D E
E E N   A A R O N   K I L O S
T D S   S P E E D   S E E M S
```

8

```
M I S E R   I C E S   D A M E
A S T R O   S H A H   A D O S
R O Y A L F L U S H   N E O S
    L E E R Y   T U L L E
S P I G O T   N A V Y B E A N
C O L O N E L   A P E
R A I D   E R A S E   R D A
A C A S E O F T H E B L U E S
P H D   A N T E S   U R N S
    A T T   O P E R A T E
S K Y D I V E R   O M E L E T
P L A I N   N O I S E
L I N D   P O W D E R P U F F
A N K A   O L D E   G E N I E
T E S S   W A Y S   E P O X Y
```

9

```
M A M M A   A D S   A B U T S
A B E A T   L E T   N E P A L
T E R R A   T A I   T A S T Y
A L V I N T O F F L E R
    N E O   F E N   T L C
S I M O N W I E S E N T H A L
E M O   D I V A   A R O M A
D I O R   T E R M S   I M A M
A G R E E   L O T T   A Z O
T H E O D O R E D R E I S E R
E T D   W W I   E R N
    T H E C H I P M U N K S
A T A R I   H A N   I R E N E
R O G E T   E S T   T E H E E
M O O S E   R H O   E D I E S
```

10

```
O N C E   I D E A L   F A S T
L E I A   R E T R O   O N T O
D O N T B E A S T R A N G E R
    M U D D   E N D Z O N E
P A V E S   E S S E S   L O U
A T E   B N A I   R A S P
C A E S A R   R A D I O
  D R O P I N A N Y T I M E
  L T C O L   A O L E R S
L O G O   B E I N   N A P
A L A   T I L E S   B O S S Y
W E L F A R E   O D I N
Y A L L C O M E B A C K N O W
E R O O   N A V A L   E A R P
R Y N E   S N A R E   Y M C A
```

11

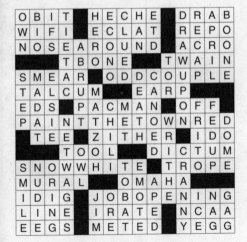

O	B	I	T		H	E	C	H	E		D	R	A	B
W	I	F	I		E	C	L	A	T		R	E	P	O
N	O	S	E	A	R	O	U	N	D		A	C	R	O
		T	B	O	N	E			T	W	A	I	N	
S	M	E	A	R		O	D	D	C	O	U	P	L	E
T	A	L	C	U	M		E	A	R	P				
E	D	S		P	A	C	M	A	N		O	F	F	
P	A	I	N	T	T	H	E	T	O	W	N	R	E	D
	T	E	E		Z	I	T	H	E	R		I	D	O
	T	O	O	L		D	I	C	T	U	M			
S	N	O	W	W	H	I	T	E		T	R	O	P	E
M	U	R	A	L		O	M	A	H	A				
I	D	I	G		J	O	B	O	P	E	N	I	N	G
L	I	N	E		I	R	A	T	E		N	C	A	A
E	E	G	S		M	E	T	E	D		Y	E	G	G

12

B	O	B	U	P		F	L	U	B		G	E	A	R
A	B	A	S	E		I	O	T	A		O	M	N	I
L	I	B	E	R	A	L	B	E	N	E	F	I	T	S
K	E	Y		F	L	I	E	S		V	E	R	S	E
			L	E	I	A			P	E	R			
R	A	D	I	C	A	L	S	I	G	N		A	L	T
A	L	E	R	T	S		M	E	A	T	S	T	E	W
I	L	I	A		O	A	R			L	A	N	A	
N	O	T	S	O	F	A	R		P	O	U	R	I	N
S	T	Y		L	E	F	T	H	A	N	G	I	N	G
		A	D	Z			A	Y	E	S				
S	T	Y	L	E		P	A	T	T	Y		H	A	T
P	R	O	G	R	E	S	S	I	V	E	L	E	N	S
I	O	W	A		L	A	I	N		A	O	R	T	A
N	Y	S	E		S	T	A	G		R	Y	D	E	R

13

S	H	A	R	P		C	A	V	E	D		P	A	T
E	A	G	E	R		A	L	E	R	O		O	L	E
C	L	O	S	E	F	R	I	E	N	D		P	A	M
			N	E	V	E	R		G	R	U	M	P	
	O	B	T	U	S	E		Z	E	A	L	O	T	
J	U	L	E	P	S		D	H	A	R	M	A		
O	T	O	E	S		H	O	O	P	S		R	B	I
K	I	S	S		C	A	R	B	S		T	B	A	R
Y	E	S		F	O	L	I	O		M	A	R	L	A
	O	L	I	V	E	S		S	A	T	E	E	N	
E	R	M	I	N	E		M	A	C	A	W	S		
M	I	T	Z	I		O	H	A	R	A				
E	L	O		C	O	M	I	C	A	B	B	O	T	T
N	E	B		K	N	A	C	K		R	E	T	R	O
D	Y	E		Y	A	N	K	S		E	A	T	U	P

The missing word is BUD.

14

L	A	C	Y		A	D	M	I	T		D	I	K	E
O	B	I	E		R	E	I	N	S		E	R	L	E
B	U	T	T	H	A	T	S	N	O	T	F	A	I	R
E	T	E		A	R	E	S			O	A	T	E	S
			C	H	A	R		N	U	T	M	E	G	
O	L	D	H	A	T		B	A	S	I	E			
M	O	R	E		A	R	D	E	N		V	I	A	
E	V	E	R	Y	O	N	E	I	S	G	O	I	N	G
N	E	W		O	R	D	E	R		W	E	R	E	
	L		G	U	A	R	D		S	P	E	W	E	D
	L	I	A	B	L	E		B	A	L	D			
L	O	R	R	E		H	I	Y	A		D	U	O	
I	C	A	N	T	D	O	A	N	Y	T	H	I	N	G
P	A	N	E		S	U	R	G	E		E	M	I	R
S	L	I	T		L	I	M	O	S		P	E	T	E

15

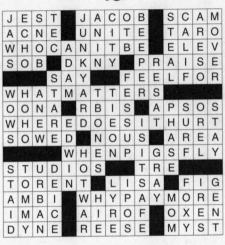

J	E	S	T		J	A	C	O	B		S	C	A	M
A	C	N	E		U	N	I	T	E		T	A	R	O
W	H	O	C	A	N	I	T	B	E		E	L	E	V
S	O	B		D	K	N	Y		P	R	A	I	S	E
			S	A	Y		F	E	E	L	F	O	R	
W	H	A	T	M	A	T	T	E	R	S				
O	O	N	A		R	B	I	S		A	P	S	O	S
W	H	E	R	E	D	O	E	S	I	T	H	U	R	T
S	O	W	E	D		N	O	U	S		A	R	E	A
			W	H	E	N	P	I	G	S	F	L	Y	
S	T	U	D	I	O	S		T	R	E				
T	O	R	E	N	T		L	I	S	A		F	I	G
A	M	B	I		W	H	Y	P	A	Y	M	O	R	E
I	M	A	C		A	I	R	O	F		O	X	E	N
D	Y	N	E		R	E	E	S	E		M	Y	S	T

16

```
HAFTS ■ WAGE ■ ADZE
ARLEN ■ OVAL ■ IRON
JOYEUXNOEL ■ REOS
IMBIBE ■ CASABA ■
■ AYN ■ NRA ■ LAMPS
■ GLAEDELIGJUL
ARGUE ■ DOSO ■ ORU
BIOPICS ■ PLUMBER
ADD ■ NEER ■ MUSES
FELIZNAVIDAD ■
TRINI ■ ETA ■ BAM
■ NETMEN ■ REAPED
ELEV ■ BUONNATALE
DOSE ■ ARFS ■ SHREK
USSR ■ SOFA ■ ESTEE
```

17

```
ABBA ■ DRIVE ■ LOAN
COEN ■ EATEN ■ OPIE
HEADINTHECLOUDS
ERN ■ RISER ■ ASSET
■ TAR ■ ONE ■
HEARTOFDARKNESS
ALBEE ■ LAITY ■ NAT
REOS ■ FOURH ■ ANTI
SNO ■ TOWNE ■ BRUIN
HANDSONTRAINING
■ OLD ■ TKO ■
CARGO ■ SUITE ■ ASK
HEALTHINSURANCE
ERIE ■ ADDON ■ STAG
WONG ■ LEONE ■ HERS
```

18

```
ICON ■ SCTV ■ OCCAM
CUBA ■ CRUE ■ RHETT
BRIM ■ OUST ■ WOOLS
METEORSHOWER ■
■ TACO ■ ELAPSE
■ WEATHERBALLOON
RIDGE ■ AER ■ ECUA
EMI ■ SHUTEYE ■ ORC
APTS ■ USE ■ AMNOT
CLOUDFORMATION ■
TERRIF ■ ASSN ■
■ FLYINGSAUCER
CILIA ■ MUNI ■ SIZE
ARENT ■ ADES ■ ETRE
BADGE ■ YETI ■ SEAL
```

19

```
GALAS ■ VOCAL ■ IRS
ALANA ■ AISLE ■ VIC
ZESTFORLIFE ■ OVA
ACHIEVE ■ ASTRAL
■ RASCAL ■ KYLE
TACO ■ LEADFOOT ■
EXODUS ■ MOAT ■ ORC
CLASS ■ LES ■ RAWER
HES ■ EZIO ■ GAZEBO
■ TODIEFOR ■ TRAP
OLGA ■ PUFFIN ■
COURIC ■ NEONGAS
TRA ■ TONEOFVOICE
ERR ■ ADEPT ■ ALLOW
TED ■ RETIE ■ SOAPS
```

20

```
SEEP ■ OKLA ■ CHASE
HULA ■ NAIL ■ LOGIN
OBIT ■ ERNE ■ ERODE
WIZ ■ LANECHANGES
SEA ■ ALA ■ ONE ■
■ BET ■ KENTSTATE
CREPES ■ LODE ■ DAB
RATA ■ CHINO ■ DATA
ASH ■ RHOS ■ GERMAN
WHITELIES ■ REA ■
■ UTE ■ ERA ■ NAP
DAILYPLANET ■ DIE
ASCAP ■ ALAS ■ MEMO
STONE ■ DOTE ■ OVEN
HONED ■ STET ■ WEDS
```

21

```
F A N G S # C L A S S # F L O
A D E A L # Y A H O O # L I Z
B O W L I N G B A L L # A L A
# A M I N O # O S K A R # # #
T A P # T U R T L E N E C K #
E L A P S E S # A I D A # # #
N O V A E # E P A # R O M A #
T H E Y C A N B E R O L L E D
S A S H # M O B # W E D G E #
# I D O L # S U N D I A L # #
Q U A K E R O A T S # E N E #
U N D E R # D E M O S # # # #
A T A # M O V I E C A M E R A
R I G # A R I E L # F U M E S
T E E # L O C U S # S T U D S
```

22

```
P A L E # O G E E # A M B E R
E L E E # R U L E # L O O S E
P A R K E D I L L E G A L L Y
S R O # N E D # # L I T # # #
I M I N T R O U B L E # H E P
# O R S # N A I R # O X O
E M O R Y # D R E S C H E R #
M A R M # H E R B S # H O C K
C R E A T U R E # B O S S Y #
E C O # I R I S # P E R # # #
E O S # P R E S S A G E N T S
# U S A # P R E # I I I
L E N G T H Y M E E T I N G S
O V U L E # E B A N # M E R S
S A T Y R # P A R T # P R E Y
```

23

```
M E D A L # E G A D # A S I F
A L E X A # M O L E # F A T E
R E M E M B E R P R O F I L E
A N O # B O R I S # M O L L S
T A C T # N I L # S I R # # #
# R E C O L L E C T D U S T #
G L A R E # A K A # S O U #
O A T M E A L # G R A M M A R
E M I # B A M # L E A R N #
R E C A L L W A I T I N G # #
# C U E # R N A # S A G O
C L A R A # T A C I T # Z E N
R E C O U N T C A L O R I E S
A G E S # B O A S # M A N S E
B O D S # A P S E # S W E E T
```

24

```
Y I P S # L E E J # G L A R E
A R I A # O B L A # O O Z E S
K A T Y # G R A F # S Q U A T
O N T H E G O L F C O U R S E
V I S I N E # A L F A # # #
# L R O N # A T C O S T
S E L M A # L O R N # I N T O
P L A Y I N G E I G H T E E N
A L U M # Y A N G # E Y I N G
R A D I A L # D A W G # # #
# S L O E # R E V I S E
H I T T I N G T H E L I N K S
A S I A N # R A I N # L O I S
S T A K E # E X E C # L I L A
H O S E D # T I S H # A L L Y
```

25

```
R O A M # E L I N O R # C U B
E U R O # D E R I V E # O L E
H I N D Q U A R T E R # R N A
A J A # U A R # T R U D E A U
B A Z A A R # J I T N E Y # #
# V I D E O # I S T H M I
C R U E L # T H O M # S A I D
H O N # S C A N N E D # R K O
A B C D # A L D A # H A T E S
S O L E M N # O N T A P # #
# E L O I S E # A R E N A S
L A B T E S T # A I M # O R E
A P U # S T A G F L A T I O N
M I C # H E R E T O # E S S O
P A K # A R R E A R # D E E R
```

26

```
H A D   T H E M A   S K I E D
O B I   S O N A R   H I T M E
B L A C K J A C K   A N S O N
N A L A   O C A   O D E S
O R I N G   T W O F O R O N E
B E N D E R S   V F W   Y A Y
    I R E   M E R   P O U R
G O L D E N P A R A C H U T E
I D E E   T E X   M O O
B E E   E A R   S P O T T E R
B A J I L L I O N   P O I S E
    C H A S   R O N   I N C A
G O O E Y   A G O O D D E A L
U R B A N   H A Z E S   A P T
S A B R E   S N E L L   R E Y
```

27

```
L E T E M   C E L E B   D A D
I L O N A   E N V O Y   A D O
M A N S T A N D I N G   N O G
O N E N E S S   U S I N G
    D A Y S O F P O M P E I I
B E E R   T R O O P   E L S E
I T A L O   O L E I C
O A F   T H E L A S T   N A Y
    A T A R I   S T O N E
B O S C   R O S S I   E T N A
O F T H E M O H I C A N S
G L E E M   T E N D O N S
I A N   P I C T U R E S H O W
E T O   T O P U P   S T O R E
S E G   Y U L E S   T O T I E
```

28

```
A M I S S   C R A M   F A Z E
R E C A P   L O N E   U R A L
E L I T E   O U T S   N I P S
T O N Y C U R T I S   N A S A
E N G R   S O S   K A Y
    M E X   D I S C M A N
M A P P E D   S E T P I E C E
I D I O T   N Y C   E D G E D
C A N N A B I S   K N E A D S
A R G Y L E S   B E S
    C S I   S E E   S T O P
A Q U A   J O H N N Y C A K E
B U R R   I T O O   M O L A R
L I S T   N O T I   C R O P S
E T A S   G E S T   A N N I E
```

29

```
C H I T A   L A P D   S P C A
H O P I S   A T L I   I R O N
A G O N Y   I R A N   C O N N
    C L A R I N E T   F D A
H O T T U B   A B R A S I O N
U N E   M O T   O C A T
L I N E   R O L O   I S E R E
C O N N E C T A L L T H E O S
E N I D S   O T O E   A R M S
    S A T O   F O B   E E E
F O S T E R E D   V E R D O N
A C H   R E L A T I V E
U H O H   I D L E   E N O L A
N O E S   D E A N   L E N O X
A S S T   A R I D   S W E L L
```

The four lines form an O-BOW ("oboe").

30

```
C A R   D A L A I   S P L A T
H O O   I M E A N   O M E G A
A R M   S I G H T U N S E E N
S T I N G   S A N T
M A J O R I N   C L A M B A R
S E N S A T E   T V G U I D E
        C A T S   I L I E
W H O L E W H E A T B R E A D
I O L A   C L U E
T H E H U T U   I N T O T A L
T O O R D E R   F E R R A R I
    D R A T   O R R I N
S H I N E A L I G H T   R A N
A M O U R   I R I S H   E N E
P O U T S   C E L T S   D A Y
```

31

```
W A D E S . A F R O . A B B A
A D O B E . Z E E S . T E A S
D E R A T . T A L C . L A S H
. M Y S T E R Y A L A S K A .
P A R . A E C . R O S T E R .
I G O T I T . S O I L . S T P
P R O B L E M C H I L D . . .
S A M S . I O N . A L I T . .
. P U Z Z L E P A L A C E . .
I M A . N E E D . A R I S E N
F A R O U T . S T R . T D S .
E N I G M A M A C H I N E . .
V I O L . P A R E . V E X E D
E L S E . S T A N . A V I S O
R A I D . I S L E . L E T O N
```

32

```
S O T O . E R O S . M I R O S
T H R U . X O U T . A B O R T
I M I T . A C R E . R I S K Y
P A T R I C K S W A Y Z E . .
E N T E N T E . C L A M P S .
. A N A T H E M A . A L E .
S P I C . E V E N . R A E .
M I C H A E L M A S D A I S Y
A P E . T B S P . . F E M A .
R E P . H O U S E C A T . . .
T R A J A N . C A M E L O T .
. L A Z Y H A Z Y C R A Z Y .
I V A N A . A H E M . A N O N
D E C I R . R O M A . L A N A
S T E E D . D Y A N . L I E N
```

33

```
P A L E T T E . B O B C A T S
A G O N I E S . O N E I D A S
K E G G E R S . L E G G I N G
. A R P E G G I O . A G T .
A M I G O S . R E F R Y . .
L I M E D . M I R . R O E S
O S E . Y A Z . N A R N I A
H A L F . D O Z E N . E G G S
A D D E R S . L O W . I M F
. D A T A . M I N . S A N A A
. A M E A N . I L L E S T .
A P U . P E G G Y S U E . .
B E G G A R Y . V E G G I E S
M A L A R I A . E N G A R D E
S K I T T E R . S T O R E U P
```

34

```
B O A T . M C K A Y . E G G O
A H S O . P H I L O . C L A P
S N I P . H O L L O W S U I T
S O F T Y . I N F . E T O N S
. H E I R . O C E A N S .
H I R I N G S Q U A D S .
A R I S T O . U R L . Y I P E
H O N . L O S E S I T . B O A
A C D C . F I S . B A K E R S
. H E E D T H E K I T T Y .
. G R A N D E . O R E S .
C L A I R . W A N . I S L A M
H A I R Y T A L E S . O I L Y
E R S E . B L I S S . F L A T
R E E D . S K A T E . F I S H
```

35

```
S O U P . P A N S Y . A C N E
A R N O . I L E N E . C O U P
C L A W . S T R I N G T R I O
R O P E . C O O P . P I N T S
E N T R I E S . C O O S .
. . . S S S . F R A . N A P E
S O D A S . B L O T S . L A D
T H E W H O L E S H E B A N G
D H S . E R I C A . W E D G E
S I K H . T P K . J E T . .
. C O T S . A E R A T O R
H U L A S . C U T S . T O P E
O P E R A R O L E S . R Y A N
W O R D . E R A S E . O O R T
I N K S . V E N T S . N U T S
```

36

```
S H A R D   W E B B   C O M B
L I V E R   I S E E   R O A R
A L I N E   S A L E   E Z R A
M O V E A T H I G H S P E E D
      M A E     I L E
K I N D O F D R I V E   T A I
A M O U N T   H O E D   A D D
R A S H   G I N   B R A T
A G E   A D E N   M I A S M A
T E D   N O T O N E T H I N G
      A N G     I N S
P A R T O F A N A D D R E S S
A C H E   O T I C   O U T T O
A R E A   O M N I   N I T E R
R E A M   D E A N   E N A T E
```

37

```
R I T E   O B O E   O R B I T
O R A L   W I N G   B E E P S
T A L K I N G T O   T A H O E
O N C O M E T O N C U P I D
        P R O     A S S N
A L O H A   P A D R E   D E S
R E V O L T   G I A   A B L Y
O N A G A I N O F F A G A I N
M I L S   R E G   E V E R S O
A N O   M E D O C   A S S A D
      F O T O     A R T
  O F F O F F B R O A D W A Y
E M I T S   A L L O R N O N E
P A C E S   N O O K   A N N A
A R E N A   S G T S   S T I R
```

38

```
S P A M S   J A G S   A R K S
P E T A L   A C R E   C I A O
E R I C A   L A I D   E T T A
C I T Y S T A T E A N D Z I P
      S H I P   S K Y   Y E S
U P I     R E D E A L T
S U B P O E N A   O E S T E
E M A I L D O M A I N N A M E
D A R E D   M I N S T R E L
      S P I D E R S   A N Y
A B A   A G E   B U N T
G O D B L E S S A M E R I C A
A X L E   T A L L   R I V A L
Z E A L   I D O L   T B I R D
E D I T   T E E S   S E E Y A
```

39

```
D A F T   O V E N   L O S I N
O L L A   N E M O   A C H O O
E V E R Y E N T R Y T H A T S
S A X   I L E S   A I R W A Y
      S P E E   A C N E
I N T H E G R I D H A S T H E
D A W E S   N I T   R E N
E N O S   S P I T S   M O S T
A N A   O A T   M O U S E
S A M E F I R S T L E T T E R
      S I R E   V A S E
B U S T L E   A T R A   A R M
A S T H E E N T R Y S C L U E
R E L E T   C A A N   A B E T
O D O R S   O N Y X   T A S S
```

40

```
F O B S   A S P S   R A K E S
A B I E   L I E U   I W E R E
C O R A L E X A M   B E L I E
T E D   A R T S   C R E S T S
    C O N T H E L O O K O U T
L E A V E S     O P A
U G L I   B O E R S   W A S
C O L D F O L K S A T H O M E
E N S   A C I D S   A L E X
      R E N   P A N F R Y
C O I L P A I N T I N G S
A S S O O N   O E N O   B E L
U T E R I   C O V E N W A R E
S A R A N   A N Y A   S N O G
A R E N T   P E E L   J E S S
```

41

A	T	O	P		A	P	S	E		A	L	M	S	
R	O	U	E		N	I	C	E		R	E	A	P	
M	O	R	T	O	N	S	A	L	T	G	I	R	L	
	S	H	I	A	T	S	U			Y	E	W		
A	R	C	H	I	E			T	E	E	P	E	E	
W	A	H	O	O		J	A	R		A	T	O	N	E
A	S	A	P		F	I	R	E	T	R	A	P		
Y	A	M		P	E	N	G	U	I	N		P	A	W
	B	L	U	E	N	O	S	E		T	I	L	E	
G	R	E	E	R		I	N	E		M	O	N	E	T
B	E	R	G	E	N			H	O	U	S	E	S	
S	A	L		A	N	X	I	O	U	S				
	C	A	R	R	Y	U	M	B	R	E	L	L	A	S
	T	I	N	E		D	A	I	S		E	A	S	T
	S	N	A	G		E	S	S	E		S	O	S	A

42

A	T	L	A	S		T	E	A	R		D	A	R	C
T	R	I	N	E		E	N	N	E		E	G	A	L
T	I	N	K	E	R	T	O	Y	S		N	O	N	O
N	O	A	H	S	A	R	K		T	B	I	R	D	S
			T	A	I	L	O	R	M	A	D	E		
B	E	A	U	S			E	R	O	S				
A	G	G	R	O		S	L	E	E	K		S	I	S
J	O	H	N	L	E	C	A	R	R	E	B	O	O	K
A	S	A		I	G	O	R	S		I	R	A	N	I
			E	C	R	U			N	A	K	E	D	
S	O	L	D	I	E	R	B	O	Y					
A	W	A	I	T	S		O	P	E	D	P	A	G	E
M	E	S	S		S	P	Y	C	A	M	E	R	A	S
O	N	T	O		E	R	E	I		A	T	I	L	T
A	S	S	N		S	O	R	T		J	E	S	S	E

43

A	B	S	O	R	B	S		T	H	E	B	L	O	B
T	E	Q	U	I	L	A		S	U	N	R	I	S	E
R	E	I	T	M	A	N		U	G	L	I	E	S	T
A	N	N		E	N	D	E	R		E	N	O	S	
		A	S	K		P	I	L	A	F				
S	I	L	L		Y	E	S	E	S		R	E	I	
T	R	E	A	S	U	R	E		I	S	L	A	N	D
P	A	T	R	O	N	S		S	C	O	U	R	G	E
A	N	I	M	A	L		C	R	A	C	K	E	R	S
T	I	N		V	I	T	U	S		E	R	S	T	
		B	E	T	H	S		C	B	S				
O	H	S	O		O	S	C	A	R		F	I	B	
R	E	P	O	M	A	N		A	V	A	R	I	C	E
B	L	A	Z	I	N	G		S	A	D	D	L	E	S
S	P	R	E	A	D	S		S	E	S	A	M	E	S

44

S	P	A	R	S		O	T	C		O	C	H	S	
P	I	N	A	T	A		R	O	A	D	J	A	C	K
A	R	I	S	E	S		A	E	R	I	A	L	L	Y
C	A	M	P	A	I	G	N	T	R	A	I	L		
E	T	A		M	A	R		A	Y	N		E	W	E
S	E	L	F		A	V	G		S	D	A	K		
		L	Y	N	N	E		M	E	K	O	N	G	
G	R	O	U	N	D	R	U	N	N	I	N	G		
O	L	E	O	L	E		S	N	O	O	D			
J	A	G	R		S	E	A			S	O	L	E	
S	D	I		A	P	O		P	S	T		P	O	D
	N	A	I	L	O	N	T	H	E	H	E	A	D	
C	O	A	L	M	I	N	E		A	V	A	N	T	I
B	U	L	L	S	E	Y	E		H	I	T	T	H	E
S	T	D	S		D	I	D		S	H	O	E	S	

45

P	A	S	S		L	A	V	A			A	F	B	S
A	W	O	L		A	D	I	N		A	T	R	I	A
B	R	A	I	N	D	E	A	D		R	O	U	E	N
L	A	M	P	O	I	L		Y	A	O	M	I	N	G
O	P	I	U	M	D	E	N		L	U	S	T		
			P	E	A		A	M	I	S		T	A	X
J	O	E	S		S	P	R	E	E		R	I	M	
A	D	V		W	I	T	S	E	N	D		E	R	A
D	I	I		A	B	E	T	S		F	E	S	S	
E	E	L		H	I	T	E		A	O	L			
	Q	U	I	Z		R	A	T	F	I	N	K	S	
A	L	U	M	N	A	E		P	O	M	P	E	I	I
L	I	E	B	E		A	P	P	L	E	T	A	R	T
L	E	E	R	S		C	E	L	L		O	L	I	O
A	N	N	A		H	W	Y	S		P	E	N	N	

46

```
S A B L E ■ G O P ■ S A L E S
A R Y A N ■ A R E ■ C L O V E
V E N U S T R A P ■ R E M I X
E N I D ■ I N N ■ C U R A T E
R A G ■ W E I G H T B O X E R
■ ■ H E E D ■ Y E S ■ ■ ■
A S T I R ■ S H E A ■ E N D S
T H E R E S A I N M Y S O U P
E Y R E ■ P L E A ■ A S F O R
■ ■ B E A ■ ■ B R E L ■ ■
I N F I E L D R U L E ■ Y T D
N O R M A L ■ A P E ■ E Z R A
C L O A K ■ Z I P U P Y O U R
A I N G E ■ A S E ■ D E N S E
S E D E R ■ X E R ■ F R E T S
```

47

```
A M I ■ L O R D ■ M O S C O W
P O R ■ O B E Y ■ A P I A R Y
P O O L S I D E ■ T E M P L E
A N N E T T E ■ C A N I T ■
L I O N ♥ ■ A D O ■ ♥ L I N E
L E N D ■ F R I A R ■ E V A H
■ ■ L E O ■ S C A T ■ E M U
A T ♥ ■ N O W ♥ H I S ■ ♥ E D
M A O ■ S L O E ■ N O S ■ ■
A M F M ■ S O N N Y ■ A B C S
H A D A ♥ ■ E S O ■ ♥ B E A T
■ I D L E D ■ R E F R A M E
T A X M A N ■ ♥ B R E A K E R
O R I E N T ■ H I L L ■ E T E
E M E N D S ■ S T E T ■ R O O
```

48

```
[SET] S S A I L ■ P S I ■ W R E N
B A L B O A ■ A L T E R E G O
A R O U N D ■ R E A D Y [SET] G O
C A P S ■ Y O K E L S ■ B O N
K N E E S ■ N A V Y ■ J U N E
■ ■ D A T I V E ■ M E T ■ ■
A R M ■ L A C E ■ H O T T E A
C E A [SET] O B E ■ H O U [SET] O P S
C D R O M S ■ C E O S ■ N I P
■ ■ Q U E ■ C H A P E L ■ ■
S H U T ■ C H A R ■ R U L E D
H O I ■ T H I R D S ■ M I N E
U N [SET] T L I N G ■ L A M B D A
N O T A C L U E ■ A D O R E D
T R E X ■ L P S ■ B O X E D [SET]
```

49

```
H U M ■ S P A S ■ O N T A P ■
O N O ■ T O D O ■ N E E S O N
A I R R A I D S ■ E R R A T A
X D O U T ■ L A N D F I G H T
E L S E ■ M E D E A ■ R O T
S E E S T O ■ S Y S T O L E
■ ■ ■ R O G E T ■ L A U E R
U S M A R I N E C O R P S ■
S N A I L ■ B E A U T ■ ■ ■
T O L D A L L ■ P S Y C H S
A P T ■ A E O N S ■ I H O P
S E A B A T T L E ■ S P O O L
I N W A N T ■ S E M P E R F I
S E A N C E ■ O D O R ■ D I T
■ D Y K E S ■ N Y N Y ■ S T S
```

50

```
S A M P L E R ■ C A R D I A C
P R A L I N E ■ O L E A N N A
A L L E R G Y ■ R A I N H A T
R E D B E A N S A N D R I C E
K N E E ■ G O A L ■ O D O R
Y E N S ■ E L K S ■ T W I N E
■ ■ ■ R I D E ■ R A N D R
I N D I A N S ■ T S O N G A S
D A U N T ■ C A H N ■ ■ ■
L I L T S ■ B A L E ■ A F R O
E L L E ■ A R K S ■ B E E P
C H A R L E S D E G A U L L E
H O R N E T S ■ D O S S I E R
A L D E N T E ■ A N T E N N A
T E S T O U T ■ T E A S E T S
```

51

I	M	P	A	S	S	E		G	A	P	E	S	A	T
L	E	A	P	T	A	T		A	D	O	L	P	H	E
L	A	G	O	O	N	S		B	I	O	M	A	S	S
S	T	O	P	I	T		U	S	E	R		N	O	T
			C	A	E	N		U	S	H				
	D	O	M		A	L	I	F		H	E	R	O	D
R	E	T	U	R	N	T	O	R	E	A	L	I	T	Y
A	L	O	T	O	N	O	N	E	S	P	L	A	T	E
C	L	E	A	R	A	N	C	E	C	E	N	T	E	R
E	A	S	T	S		S	I	L	O		O	A	R	
			E	C	O		T	Y	R	E				
A	W	L		H	A	Z	Y		T	A	T	T	L	E
P	R	E	B	A	K	E		B	I	G	H	O	A	X
P	I	E	R	C	E	D		O	N	L	E	A	V	E
S	T	J	O	H	N	S		A	G	E	N	D	A	S

52

B	E	B	O	P		C	H	I	N	R	E	S	T	S
U	V	U	L	A		A	U	D	I	O	B	O	O	K
N	A	D	E	R		E	C	O	M	M	E	R	C	E
	G	A	S	T	A	N	K		B	A	R	R	O	W
C	A	P	T	O	R			W	I	N	S	O	M	E
A	B	E	R	N	A	T	H	Y		C	O	W	E	R
S	O	S	A		G	R	E	N	D	E	L			
A	R	T		B	O	O	S	T	E	D		L	U	V
			H	A	N	G	S	O	N		V	I	S	A
A	L	T	A	R		G	E	N	T	L	E	B	E	N
S	E	A	N	C	E	S			O	A	T	E	R	S
P	A	R	D	O	N		T	A	N	N	E	R	S	
I	N	S	I	D	E	J	O	B		D	R	A	F	T
S	T	A	L	E	M	A	T	E		H	A	L	E	N
H	O	L	Y	S	Y	N	O	D		O	N	S	E	T

53

	M	I	A	M	I		E	E	L	E	D			
	J	E	N	N	I	F	E	R	L	O	P	E	Z	
L	A	N	D	O	C	A	L	R	I	S	S	I	A	N
E	N	T		S	A	T	I	A	T	E		F	D	A
T	G	I	F		S	A	O	N	E		S	I	O	N
A	L	O	A	F		L	T	D		O	P	E	R	A
T	E	N	D	R	I	L		S	A	M	O	S	A	S
			D	O	N			L	E	K				
A	S	S	I	G	N	S		P	E	G	A	S	U	S
L	U	T	E	S		A	V	I		A	N	I	S	E
A	S	E	T		P	I	A	N	O		E	D	E	N
R	I	A		R	E	L	L	E	N	O		E	T	O
M	E	M	B	E	R	S	O	F	T	H	E	B	A	R
	Q	U	I	C	K	B	R	O	W	N	F	O	X	
		P	O	T	S	Y		R	O	O	T	Y		

54

S	C	A	L	A	R				I	V	I	N	S	
E	A	S	I	N	E	S	S		C	A	N	O	E	
E	P	I	C	T	A	L	E	S		U	P	T	H	E
M	O	V	I	E	F	O	N	E		O	H	O	H	
S	T	E	A	D	F	A	S	T		C	R	E	P	E
					O	N	E	S	T	R	I	P	E	R
			W	H	E	R	E	S	T	H	E	F	I	R	E
	S	H	A	M	E	S		H	E	M	I	N	S	
S	C	A	R	E	S	T	H	E	H	E	C	K		
P	E	R	P	E	T	R	A	T	E					
I	N	F	E	R		E	M	A	I	L	L	I	S	T
K	E	R	R		E	M	B	R	O	I	D	E	R	
E	X	A	L	T		T	E	L	E	S	C	O	P	Y
T	I	T	E	R		D	E	S	C	E	N	T	S	
V	I	S	E	S			S	H	Y	E	S	T		

55

S	O	L	A	R			T	I	R	E	D	O	F	
K	N	I	F	E		O	P	E	R	A	T	I	V	E
A	T	S	E	A		M	A	L	E	M	O	D	E	L
T	H	A	W		S	E	R	E		S	N	O	R	T
E	E	K		S	Y	N	A	P	S	E	S			
	L	U	B	E	D		D	A	W	S		T	S	A
G	O	D	E	L		Z	I	T	I		S	H	I	N
M	O	R	A	L	H	I	G	H	G	R	O	U	N	D
A	S	O	K		O	N	M	Y		E	A	M	E	S
N	E	W		S	A	C	S		B	A	R	B	Q	
			Z	E	R	O	H	O	U	R		S	U	B
A	W	G	E	E		X	I	N	G		A	D	A	R
T	H	A	T	S	L	I	F	E		S	C	O	N	E
R	E	L	A	T	E	D	T	O		O	H	W	O	W
A	W	E	S	O	M	E		P	E	N	N	S		

56

```
M A G N E T I S M █ C H I C
A L L A T O N C E █ P H O N O
D O I T A G A I N █ H A M A N
E N D █ S N E A K I N E S S
█ G E T A █ E N G E L █ L E I
█ I R R █ C E Y █ N A R D
█ T H E M I S E R █ G E N I E
P I E R O G I █ I N O R D E R
O M A R R █ D R E Y F U S S █
S E R A █ B E E █ C A D █
I S T █ M I S S M █ R A H S
T H E P R O P H E T █ O W L
R A N E E █ I O N I A N S E A
O R E A D █ N O S E C O N E S
N E D S █ S T A R T W I T H
```

57

```
S A D R C I T Y █ B E I G E S
T R U E L O V E █ E L N I N O
A T A L A N T A █ E M A J O R
T I L █ M I R R O R █ R O T E
E C R U █ C A N A █ Q U E E N
S L O P E █ Y E R O U T █
M E L O T T █ D E S E █ S K Y
A V E N U E C █ D O N T L I E
N I S █ D A R E █ S C R I M S
█ C E L I C A █ H A D J I
S O N Y S █ E S T D █ P E O N
T E A R █ I S E E I T █ I N D
A S H A R P █ G A S R A N G E
I T U N E S █ A S C O T T I E
D E M O D E █ R E I N H O L D
```

58

```
A S S U A G E █ G R A P P L E
P O U R C O L D W A T E R O N
I M A G I N A R Y F R I E N D
E B B E D █ P E N T A █ N E Z
C E L S █ A S S N S █ P A S O
E R E █ E L I S E █ R A T O N
█ C R O N Y █ S E S A M E
W I S H I N G █ G E N T L E S
A C T O N E █ D I R T Y █
T E R M S █ H O F F A █ J E D
C H I P █ R U N T S █ M E M O
H O C █ R E N E W █ C I R C E
O U T R I G G E R C A N O E S
U S E D C A R S A L E S M E N
T E R S E L Y █ P I N K E S T
```

59

```
M R I S █ E G O B O O S T S
A I N T █ P A T E N T L A W
D P L U S █ O Z O N E H O L E
L E E █ T A X E S █ N E W M E
I N A N E L Y █ F I R E U P
B I G A P E █ B L O G █ R D S
S N U F F █ H A I G H T █
█ G E T O N T H E S T I C K
█ A R O M A S █ S E A N S
P R O █ D E L I █ S T O P I T
R E N E W S █ P L A N S T O
E L E M I █ D E I O N █ I T O
C A P E V E R D E █ D A Z E D
I T I N E R A N T █ J E R I
S E N D S A W A Y █ A S S N
```

60

```
P A S S E D U P █ S T U P I D
A R T U R O T O S C A N I N I
C L E R I C A L C O L L A R S
M E R G E █ H A I R L I N E S
A N N E █ C A R O N █ M O P E
N E O █ F O G I N █ N I K O N
█ N A M E S █ C U T E S T
M A D I G A N █ S A D E Y E S
C L O N E S █ D O M E D █
E G G O N █ L O C U S █ M U D
N E W T █ H U L K S █ T I L E
T R A C T A B L E █ P U N T S
I N T H E N E A R F U T U R E
R O C K A N D R O L L S T A R
E N H A L O █ S O U P I E S T
```

61

P	I	L	E	D	H	I	G	H	█	█	S	A	P	S
O	N	E	B	E	D	R	O	O	M	█	E	I	R	E
P	A	R	A	L	L	E	L	E	D	█	W	R	I	T
I	W	O	N	T	█	█	D	R	S	█	A	B	C	D
N	E	Y	█	A	R	T	E	S	█	A	G	R	E	E
█	█	█	U	S	E	O	N	█	S	E	A	T	S	█
S	C	A	R	█	S	O	P	H	I	E	█	K	A	I
W	A	L	L	S	T	L	A	Y	S	A	N	E	G	G
I	L	E	█	L	E	E	R	A	T	█	A	S	S	N
S	I	X	T	Y	█	█	A	T	L	A	W	█	█	█
S	C	A	R	E	█	O	C	T	E	T	█	R	T	S
M	O	N	A	█	I	C	H	█	█	B	A	E	R	S
A	C	D	C	█	S	H	U	T	T	E	R	B	U	G
D	A	R	E	█	R	E	T	R	O	S	P	E	C	T
E	T	A	S	█	█	R	E	A	T	T	A	C	K	S

62

B	R	E	W	S	K	I	S	█	O	N	S	I	D	E
Y	E	A	H	S	U	R	E	█	Y	A	W	N	E	R
G	A	G	O	R	D	E	R	█	S	H	A	S	T	A
O	D	E	█	S	O	N	G	█	T	A	P	E	R	S
N	O	R	D	█	S	E	I	N	E	█	S	C	A	M
E	U	L	E	R	█	S	N	E	R	D	█	T	C	U
S	T	Y	L	E	D	█	G	A	B	F	E	S	T	S
█	█	█	T	A	R	A	█	P	A	L	L	█	█	█
B	I	G	S	C	E	N	E	█	R	A	M	O	N	A
E	N	A	█	T	A	I	N	T	█	T	O	N	E	S
E	S	T	A	█	M	S	D	O	S	█	S	E	W	S
T	H	E	F	O	G	█	L	A	W	S	█	S	H	U
R	O	M	A	N	I	█	I	M	I	T	A	T	O	R
E	R	A	S	E	R	█	N	A	M	E	T	A	P	E
D	E	N	T	A	L	█	E	N	S	N	A	R	E	D

63

A	P	S	E	S	█	█	P	L	E	U	R	A	█	
B	I	L	L	E	D	█	P	E	R	A	N	N	U	M
S	P	I	D	E	R	█	O	V	E	R	T	I	M	E
C	E	P	E	D	A	█	P	A	S	S	I	T	O	N
E	S	P	R	I	T	█	A	L	T	E	R	E	R	█
S	T	A	S	E	S	█	R	U	I	N	E	R	S	█
S	E	G	O	S	█	S	T	A	G	█	█	█	█	█
█	M	E	N	T	A	L	█	T	E	S	L	A	S	█
█	█	█	C	A	B	E	█	P	O	N	E	S	█	█
█	A	C	H	I	E	V	E	█	S	A	R	T	R	E
█	M	O	U	N	T	E	R	█	A	R	R	I	V	E
T	O	P	S	C	O	R	E	█	R	E	A	P	E	R
O	N	T	H	E	N	E	T	█	A	R	I	O	S	E
C	R	E	E	P	E	R	S	█	H	I	N	D	U	S
K	A	R	S	T	S	█	█	█	B	E	E	P	S	█

64

C	A	M	P	A	N	E	L	L	A	█	Z	O	O	S
U	N	A	I	D	E	D	E	Y	E	█	I	M	U	P
T	A	S	K	M	A	S	T	E	R	█	N	A	T	L
L	G	S	█	S	L	O	T	S	█	B	E	L	L	I
E	R	A	█	O	N	E	█	M	U	S	L	I	N	█
R	A	G	L	A	N	█	R	C	A	S	█	E	N	T
S	M	E	A	R	█	E	B	O	N	Y	E	Y	E	S
█	█	█	P	E	T	S	O	U	N	D	S	█	█	█
W	I	N	D	O	W	S	X	P	█	A	T	T	I	C
I	S	O	█	L	I	E	F	█	M	Y	H	E	R	O
R	A	M	J	E	T	█	O	L	A	█	█	S	O	N
E	D	I	T	S	█	B	R	U	I	T	█	T	N	T
T	O	N	I	█	F	A	M	I	L	Y	N	A	M	E
A	R	A	L	█	U	S	A	G	E	N	O	T	E	S
P	E	L	E	█	R	E	T	I	R	E	M	E	N	T

65

H	O	T	H	E	A	D	S	█	J	J	P	U	T	Z
O	N	E	I	N	T	E	N	█	I	A	G	R	E	E
U	N	S	E	T	T	L	E	█	F	R	A	S	E	R
S	O	T	S	█	S	T	A	F	F	S	█	U	T	O
E	T	A	█	█	O	K	A	Y	█	F	L	E	E	█
S	I	B	S	█	L	I	E	D	█	B	E	A	R	D
A	C	L	U	█	O	D	D	S	A	R	E	█	█	█
T	E	E	T	H	E	█	█	█	S	A	D	I	S	T
█	█	█	R	A	W	E	G	G	S	█	E	T	E	S
M	E	D	A	L	█	L	O	I	N	█	R	H	E	A
A	X	E	S	█	E	L	I	A	█	█	I	S	R	█
S	E	S	█	P	R	A	N	C	E	█	A	N	T	I
Q	U	I	T	I	T	█	G	O	B	A	C	K	O	N
U	N	L	I	K	E	█	A	M	B	R	O	S	I	A
E	T	U	D	E	S	█	T	O	S	S	P	O	T	S

66

P	R	E	S	S	U	R	E			C	R	I	B	
R	E	L	O	A	N	E	D		P	H	O	N	O	
I	D	E	A	L	I	S	M		P	R	E	S	T	O
M	A	G	R	I	T	T	E		R	E	E	S	E	S
	S	I	E	N	E	S	E		I	N	S	E	R	T
	T	R	A	D	E	S		I	M	A	I	T	R	E
			A	E	R	O	M	E	T	E	R			
D	O	S	A	D	O	S		U	S	E	R	I	D	S
I	R	E	N	E	R	Y	A	N						
S	I	R	I	C	A		L	A	M	E	S	A		
S	E	A	M	A	N		A	B	A	S	H	E	S	
U	N	S	U	N	G		M	O	N	S	A	N	T	O
A	T	E	S	T	S		O	U	T	E	R	E	A	R
D	A	R	E	S			S	T	A	N	D	A	R	D
E	L	A	S			A	S	S	E	S	S	E	S	

67

B	U	B	B	L	E	B	A	T	H		T	W	A	S
O	P	E	R	A	S	E	R	I	A		A	I	N	T
A	D	V	A	N	C	E	M	E	N		I	N	D	O
T	O	Y	S	T	O	R	Y		D	A	C	T	Y	L
			S	E	R	S		N	O	W	H	E	R	E
H	O	B	A	R	T		F	O	U	R	I	R	O	N
A	C	O	R	N		W	I	T	T	Y		T	O	C
S	H	O	D		X	E	R	E	S		M	I	N	A
A	L	T		P	A	L	M	S		C	I	D	E	R
G	O	L	C	O	N	D	A		M	O	S	E	Y	S
O	C	E	L	O	T	S		F	O	R	T			
A	R	G	A	L	I		B	A	P	T	I	S	M	S
T	A	G	S		P	E	R	I	P	E	T	E	I	A
I	C	E	S		P	L	A	T	E	G	L	A	S	S
T	Y	R	A		E	I	G	H	T	E	E	N	T	H

68

S	K	I	N	N	Y	B	I	T	C	H		E	P	I
I	L	T	R	O	V	A	T	O	R	E		L	O	L
T	E	A	C	H	E	R	S	P	E	T		C	U	L
K	I	L		A	T	T	Y		W	E	B	A	R	T
A	N	O	I	N	T	S		S	C	R	A	P	E	R
		D	D	E		F	L	U	O	R	I	D	E	
L	O	S	E	S		B	O	A	T	S		T	O	A
A	X	I	S		T	E	X	T	S		H	A	U	T
K	Y	L		S	I	R	E	E		F	O	N	T	S
E	M	I	R	A	T	E	S		L	O	O			
T	O	C	E	L	I	A		H	A	R	D	C	A	P
A	R	A	B	I	C		E	A	S	E		R	E	A
H	O	G		N	A	S	T	Y	H	A	B	I	T	S
O	N	E		A	C	U	T	E	A	C	C	E	N	T
E	S	L		S	A	V	E	S	T	H	E	D	A	Y

69

K	I	C	K	S	T	A	R	T		S	P	L	A	T
C	L	E	O	P	A	T	R	A		P	E	A	B	O
A	L	L	C	O	M	E	R	S		E	R	N	I	E
R	E	S	H	I	P	S			D	E	F	I	E	S
			L	E	T	S	L	I	D	E				
S	C	O	R	E	R		M	T	P	O	C	O	N	O
H	E	R	O	D		R	E	G	I	S	T	R	A	R
E	D	E	L		S	A	L	O	N		T	A	D	S
R	E	A	L	I	T	Y	T	V		A	E	R	I	E
M	D	D	E	G	R	E	E		A	S	N	E	A	R
			R	O	A	D	R	A	G	E				
S	H	E	B	O	P		C	A	P	E	C	O	D	
P	I	L	A	F		F	I	R	S	T	T	A	K	E
E	F	I	L	E		R	A	I	S	I	N	P	I	E
W	I	E	L	D		I	N	D	I	C	A	T	E	D

70

A	Z	T	E	C	S		S	A	M	P	A	N	S
R	E	H	E	A	T		H	A	V	E	A	C	O	W
A	R	E	O	L	E		E	X	I	T	V	I	S	A
B	O	B		L	E	E	R		D	R	E	D	A	Y
I	Z	O	D		P	A	C	T		O	D	I	L	E
S	E	X	E	S		T	U	R	I	N		C	T	R
T	R	E	B	L	E		L	I	M	O	S			
	O	R	I	E	N	T	E	X	P	R	E	S	S	
		S	I	T	U	P		S	T	R	A	T	A	
F	G	S		G	O	G	O	L		H	I	F	I	S
L	O	A	T	H		S	I	A	M		F	E	L	L
O	N	F	I	R	E		R	Y	E	S		A	L	A
R	E	A	D	I	N	T	O		D	E	A	R	E	R
A	I	R	E	D	O	U	T		E	N	B	E	R	G
S	N	I	D	E	S	T		A	T	E	A	S	E	

71

```
C O O K I E J A R   N O R M S
O P P O R T U N E   U B O A T
R E C O V E R E D   R I O J A
E R I K   S Y M S   S E T O N
S A T Y R   B I T T E   C R I
        E C O C A R   F A D S
J U N K F A X   R E T I N O L
E N U R E S       P A J A M A
A D M I R A L   M A N I L O W
N E B S   B U S O N I
G R E   B A R Q S   A B B A S
E R R O L   C U E S   L I Z A
N A O M I   H I L L S I D E S
E T N A S   E N L A R G E R S
T E E N S   S T E V I E R A Y
```

72

```
A D E   R O L O   C O R N E R
D J S   E L O N   A R E O L A
Z I P P I E S T   J E S T E R
  B R I N G T O J U S T I C E
P O E T S   O P E N   A M T S
R U S T   A N O N   N T E S T
O T S   R E F E R E E
M I O   R E S T S O N   S T U
      P A S C H A L   T I S
A B R A M   O E I L   M A R E
D E A D   R O W S   F I R E D
V E N T R I L O Q U I S T S
I T C H E S   R U N F O R I T
S L O A N E   L O O T   E A R
E E R I E R   D I S H   K S U
```

73

```
S A R C A S M   E M P O W E R
A Q U A R I A   T E A T I M E
N U L L I T Y   I N T E R I M
J A E   D U B U Q U E   E N E
O M O O   P E R U   R A M E N
S A U N A S   B E D S T A N D
E N T E R   S A T E   O N T
    G I G A N T I S M
  S T A   E L I E   K A F I R
S C H M A L T Z   C A N A D A
P R I E D   W E A R   T R E N
I O N   R O A D B E D   S A P
C O M F O R T   I W O J I M A
E G A L I T E   D E R I D E S
S E N A T O R   E L E M E N T
```

74

```
G E T S M A D   C E R E A L S
A C E T O N E   U T E N S I L
B U R E T T E   C H A T T E R
F A R T H E R   H Y D R A S
E D I T E D   D I L   A I L S
S O N I A   O R F E   P R O W
T R E N T   P O R N O   E W E
      G E N E V I E V E
U M P   N O N E T   E X A C T
K I R S   C L I O   R I S H I
E N O L   H E N   P A S S E L
  E X O C E T   T A C T U A L
T R I P L E T   S A T I A T E
V A M O O S E   A V E N G E R
S L A N D E R   R O D G E R S
```

75

```
D A N   A S C H   E M O T E R
E L O   C H O U   D I P O L E
S A T S C O R E   U N U S E D
P R E C O O K S   C U L T I C
I M P A R T S   A T E A S E
T E A R D U C T   T E N D O N
E D D Y   P R O T E S T A N T
        E R A
B I G B A D W O L F   M U S H
A D E L I E   S L I P I N T O
R E S O R T   O N A D I E T
B A T T L E   P R E L A T E S
A M A T I S   A D A M S A L E
R E P E N T   S E R A   R I A
A N O D E S   O R T S   Y E T
```

The New York Times

Crossword Puzzles

The #1 Name in Crosswords

Available at your local bookstore or online at nytimes.com/nytstore

New This Season!

Little Luxe Book of Crosswords	0-312-38622-2
The Crossword Connoisseur	0-312-38627-3
Ready, Set, Solve! Crosswords	0-312-38623-0
Tension-Taming Crosswords	0-312-38624-9
Crosswords 101	0-312-38619-2
Large-Print Crossword Omnibus Vol. 9	0-312-38620-6
Sunday Crossword Puzzles Vol. 34	0-312-38625-7
Double Flip Book of the New York Times Crosswords and Sudoku	0-312-38635-4
Sunday Delight Crosswords	0-312-38626-5

Special Editions

1,001 Crossword Puzzles to Do Right Now	0-312-38253-7
Crosswords to Keep Your Brain Young	0-312-37658-8
Little Black (and White) Book of Crosswords	0-312-36105-X
The Joy of Crosswords	0-312-37510-7
Little Red and Green Book of Crosswords	0-312-37661-8
Little Flip Book of Crosswords	0-312-37043-1
How to Conquer the New York Times Crossword Puzzle	0-312-36554-3
Will Shortz's Favorite Crossword Puzzles	0-312-30613-X
Will Shortz's Favorite Sunday Crossword Puzzles	0-312-32488-X
Will Shortz's Greatest Hits	0-312-34242-X
Will Shortz Presents Crosswords for 365 Days	0-312-36121-1
Will Shortz's Funniest Crossword Puzzles	0-312-32489-8
Will Shortz's Funniest Crossword Puzzles Vol. 2	0-312-33960-7
Will Shortz's Xtreme Xwords	0-312-35203-4
Vocabulary Power Crosswords	0-312-35199-2

Daily Crosswords

Fitness for the Mind Crosswords Vol. 2	0-312-35278-6
Fitness for the Mind Crosswords Vol. 1	0-312-34955-6
Crosswords for the Weekend	0-312-34332-9
Daily Crossword Puzzles Vol. 72	0-312-35260-3
Daily Crossword Puzzles Vol. 71	0-312-34858-4

Daily Crossword Puzzles Volumes 57–70 also available.

Easy Crosswords

Easy Crossword Puzzles Vol. 9	0-312-37831-9
Easy Crossword Puzzles Vol. 8	0-312-36558-6
Easy Crossword Puzzles Vol. 7	0-312-35261-1

Easy Crossword Puzzles Volumes 2–6 also available.

Tough Crosswords

Tough Crossword Puzzles Vol. 13	0-312-34240-3
Tough Crossword Puzzles Vol. 12	0-312-32442-1
Tough Crossword Puzzles Vol. 11	0-312-31456-6

Tough Crossword Puzzles Volumes 9–10 also available.

Sunday Crosswords

Sunday in the Sand Crosswords	0-312-38269-3
Simply Sunday Crosswords	0-312-34243-8
Sunday in the Park Crosswords	0-312-35197-6
Sunday Morning Crossword Puzzles	0-312-35672-2
Everyday Sunday Crossword Puzzles	0-312-36106-8
Sunday Brunch Crosswords	0-312-36557-8
Sunday at the Seashore Crosswords	0-312-37070-9
Sleepy Sunday Crossword Puzzles	0-312-37508-5
Sunday's Best	0-312-37637-5
Sunday at Home Crosswords	0-312-37834-3
Sunday Crossword Puzzles Vol. 33	0-312-37507-7
Sunday Crossword Puzzles Vol. 32	0-312-36066-5
Sunday Crossword Puzzles Vol. 31	0-312-34862-2

Large-Print Crosswords

Large-Print Big Book of Holiday Crosswords	0-312-33092-8
Large-Print Crosswords for a Brain Workout	0-312-32612-2
Large-Print Crosswords for Your Coffee Break	0-312-33109-6
Large-Print Will Shortz's Favorite Crossword Puzzles	0-312-33959-3
Large-Print Crosswords to Boost Your Brainpower	0-312-32037-X
Large-Print Daily Crossword Puzzles Vol. 2	0-312-33111-8
Large-Print Daily Crossword Puzzles	0-312-31457-4
Large-Print Crosswords for Your Bedside	0-312-34245-4
Large-Print Big Book of Easy Crosswords	0-312-33958-5
Large-Print Easy Crossword Omnibus Vol. 1	0-312-32439-1
Large-Print Crossword Puzzle Omnibus Vol. 8	0-312-37514-X
Large-Print Crossword Puzzle Omnibus Vol. 7	0-312-36125-4
Large-Print Crossword Puzzle Omnibus Vol. 6	0-312-34861-4

Omnibus

Weekend in the Country	0-312-38270-7
Crosswords for Two	0-312-37830-0
Crosswords for a Relaxing Weekend	0-312-37829-7
Easy to Not-So-Easy Crossword Puzzle Omnibus Vol. 2	0-312-37832-7
Easy to Not-So-Easy Crossword Omnibus Vol. 1	0-312-37516-6
Crosswords for a Lazy Afternoon	0-312-33108-8
Lazy Weekend Crossword Puzzle Omnibus	0-312-34247-0
Lazy Sunday Crossword Puzzle Omnibus	0-312-35279-4
Big Book of Holiday Crosswords	0-312-33533-4
Giant Book of Holiday Crosswords	0-312-34927-0
Ultimate Crossword Omnibus	0-312-31622-4

Tough Crossword Puzzle Omnibus Vol. 1	0-312-32441-3
Crossword Challenge	0-312-33951-8
Crosswords for a Weekend Getaway	0-312-35198-4
Biggest Beach Crossword Omnibus	0-312-35667-6
Weekend Away Crossword Puzzle Omnibus	0-312-35669-2
Weekend at Home Crossword Puzzle Omnibus	0-312-35670-6
Holiday Cheer Crossword Puzzles	0-312-36126-2
Crosswords for a Long Weekend	0-312-36560-8
Crosswords for a Relaxing Vacation	0-312-36694-9
Will Shortz Presents Fun in the Sun Crossword Puzzle Omnibus	0-312-37041-5
Sunday Crossword Omnibus Vol. 9	0-312-35666-8
Sunday Crossword Omnibus Vol. 8	0-312-32440-5
Sunday Crossword Omnibus Vol. 7	0-312-30950-3
Easy Crossword Puzzle Omnibus Vol. 6	0-312-38287-1
Easy Crossword Puzzle Omnibus Vol. 5	0-312-36123-8
Easy Crossword Puzzle Omnibus Vol. 4	0-312-34859-2
Crossword Puzzle Omnibus Vol. 16	0-312-36104-1
Crossword Puzzle Omnibus Vol. 15	0-312-34856-8
Crossword Puzzle Omnibus Vol. 14	0-312-33534-2
Supersized Book of Easy Crosswords	0-312-35277-8
Supersized Book of Sunday Crosswords	0-312-36122-X

Previous volumes also available.

Variety Puzzles

Acrostic Puzzles Vol. 10	0-312-34853-3
Acrostic Puzzles Vol. 9	0-312-30949-X
Sunday Variety Puzzles	0-312-30059-X

Portable Size Format

The Puzzlemaster's Choice	0-312-38271-5
In the Kitchen Crosswords	0-312-38259-6
Think Outside the Box Crosswords	0-312-38261-8
Big Book of Easy Crosswords	0-312-38268-5
Real Simple Crosswords	0-312-38254-5
Crosswords by the Bay	0-312-38267-7
Crosswords for Your Coffee Break	0-312-28830-1
Sun, Sand and Crosswords	0-312-30076-X
Weekend Challenge	0-312-30079-4
Crosswords for the Holidays	0-312-30603-2
Crosswords for the Work Week	0-312-30952-X
Crosswords for Your Beach Bag	0-312-31455-8
Crosswords to Boost Your Brainpower	0-312-32033-7
Cuddle Up with Crosswords	0-312-37636-7
C Is for Crosswords	0-312-37509-3
Crazy for Crosswords	0-312-37513-1
Crosswords for a Mental Edge	0-312-37069-5
Favorite Day Crosswords: Tuesday	0-312-37072-5
Afternoon Delight Crosswords	0-312-37071-7
Crosswords Under the Covers	0-312-37044-X
Crosswords for the Beach	0-312-37073-3
Will Shortz Presents I Love Crosswords	0-312-37040-7
Will Shortz Presents Crosswords to Go	0-312-36695-7
Favorite Day Crosswords: Monday	0-312-36556-X
Crosswords in the Sun	0-312-36555-1
Expand Your Mind Crosswords	0-312-36553-5
After Dinner Crosswords	0-312-36559-4
Groovy Crossword Puzzles from the '60s	0-312-36103-3
Piece of Cake Crosswords	0-312-36124-6
Carefree Crosswords	0-312-36102-5
Fast and Easy Crossword Puzzles	0-312-35629-3
Backyard Crossword Puzzles	0-312-35668-4
Easy Crossword Puzzles for Lazy Hazy Crazy Days	0-312-35671-4
Brainbuilder Crosswords	0-312-35276-X
Stress-Buster Crosswords	0-312-35196-8
Super Saturday Crosswords	0-312-30604-0
Café Crosswords	0-312-34854-1
Crosswords for Your Lunch Hour	0-312-34857-6
Easy as Pie Crossword Puzzles	0-312-34331-0
Crosswords to Soothe Your Soul	0-312-34244-6
More Quick Crosswords	0-312-34246-2
Beach Blanket Crosswords	0-312-34250-0
Crosswords to Beat the Clock	0-312-33954-2
Crosswords for a Rainy Day	0-312-33952-6
Crosswords for Stress Relief	0-312-33953-4
Cup of Crosswords	0-312-33955-0
Crosswords to Exercise Your Brain	0-312-33536-9
Crosswords for Your Breakfast Table	0-312-33535-0
More Crosswords for Your Bedside	0-312-33612-8
T.G.I.F. Crosswords	0-312-33116-9
Quick Crosswords	0-312-33114-2
Planes, Trains and Crosswords	0-312-33113-4
More Sun, Sand and Crosswords	0-312-33112-6
Crosswords for a Brain Workout	0-312-32610-6
A Cup of Tea Crosswords	0-312-32435-9
Crosswords for Your Bedside	0-312-32032-9
Coffee Break Crosswords	0-312-37515-8
Rise and Shine Crossword Puzzles	0-312-37833-5
Coffee, Tea or Crosswords	0-312-37828-9
Will Shortz Presents I Love Crosswords Vol. 2	0-312-37837-8
Sweet Dreams Crosswords	0-312-37836-X

Other volumes also available.

St. Martin's Griffin